Lake Erie Fishermen

Lake Erie Fishermen

Work, Identity, and Tradition

Timothy C. Lloyd

and

Patrick B. Mullen

University of Illinois Press
Urbana and Chicago

© 1990 by the Board of Trustees of the University of Illinois
Manufactured in the United States of America
C 5 4 3 2 1

This book is printed on acid-free paper.

Library of Congress Cataloging-in-Publication Data

Lloyd, Timothy Charles.
  Lake Erie fishermen : work, tradition, and identity / Timothy C.
Lloyd and Patrick B. Mullen.
      p.   cm.
  Bibliography: p.
  Includes index.
  ISBN 0-252-01662-9 (alk. paper)
  1. Fishers—Erie, Lake—History. 2. Fishing—Erie, Lake—History.
I. Mullen, Patrick B., 1941-   . II. Title.
  HD8039.F66U478   1990
305.9′6392—dc20   89-35126
                                                          CIP

Contents

Acknowledgments

The fieldwork on which this book is based was supported by the Folk Arts Program of the National Endowment for the Arts in Washington, D.C. (grant 32-5530-00009) and the Ohio Sea Grant College Program of the Ohio State University in Columbus (grant NA81AA-D-00095; project R/SP-2-PD). We thank Bess Lomax Hawes, Director of the Folk Arts Program, and both Ed Herdendorf, former Director, and Jeff Reutter, Director, of the Ohio Sea Grant College Program and Ohio State University's Center for Lake Erie Area Research for their support, assistance, and helpful advice. The Ohio Sea Grant College Program and the Ohio State University College of Humanities, Micheal G. Riley, Dean, have also supported the publication of the photographs in this volume.

The Ohio Arts Council, through its executive director, Wayne Lawson, and its deputy director, Susan Neumann, and the Department of English of the Ohio State University, through its chairman Morris Beja, generously supported our work throughout this project and provided a number of helpful administrative, clerical, and fiscal services to us. The Ohio Arts Council has also supported the cost of providing copies of this book to the Lake Erie fishermen with whom we worked on this project.

Dr. Mark Barnes, a fisheries biologist working at Ohio State at the time our fieldwork began, introduced us to the many fishermen he had met in the course of his own research, patiently answered our beginners' questions, and drafted the section of the introduction on the history of commercial fishing on Lake Erie. Linda Milligan indexed all of our fieldwork tapes. Transcription of the tapes was done by

Executive Services, Inc., of Columbus. Anyone who has indexed or transcribed as many hours of tape as Linda and ESI did will appreciate their contributions. Gretchen Furlow of the Department of English typed part of the final manuscript, and Heather J. Williams corrected the final disk copy based on the copyediting of Barbara E. Cohen. Mike Szczepanik of the College of Humanities provided invaluable assistance on word processing and computers in the preparation of the manuscript.

Ohio Sea Grant College Program Communicator Margaret Holland led us through what for us was the unfamiliar process of applying for grants in the sciences, and her successor, Maran Brainard, has provided helpful editorial advice.

The late Ray Full of the Kishman Fish Company in Vermilion, the Great Lakes Historical Society of Vermilion, Jerry Hosko of Port Clinton, Jim Van Hoose of the Port Clinton Fish Company, the late Kenny Wahl of Sandusky, and George Wakefield of Vermilion all gave us access to their valuable personal or institutional collections of photographs of the area fishery, as well as much needed help and advice. Many of the photographs in Jerry Hosko's collection were taken by staff photographers from the *Toledo Blade,* and we appreciate the *Blade*'s permission to use them. Carl Baker of the Ohio Department of Natural Resources in Sandusky introduced us to the state's policies and procedures regarding the Lake Erie fishery and the commercial industry. Emily King of the Division of Watercraft assisted us in photographing a trap-net boat operation. The map of the western Lake Erie region was designed and drawn by Dan Wagner of Columbus.

A number of folklorists—most notably Charley Camp, Tim Cochrane, Janet Gilmore, Paula Johnson, Jim Leary, Jens Lund, E. Jean M. MacLaughlin, Bob McCarl, David A. Taylor, and Mark Workman—have given us advice, support, criticism, and bibliographic references throughout this project. Jens and David were particularly helpful on the bibliographic end. Bob Byington and Sandy Ives read the manuscript closely and carefully for the University of Illinois Press and helped shape the final form of the book. Bob Byington provided especially good advice on the structure and focus of the study. Judy McCulloh of the University of Illinois Press gave us support and encouragement at the point we needed it most. Ohio State University folklorists Dan Barnes and Amy Shuman have also given us advice and support. As is customary (and correct) to point out, this volume owes much to all of them, but its faults should not be construed as theirs.

Our wives—Diane Nance Lloyd and Roseanne Rini—have, as always, been our best supporters and collaborators. We would like to think that the time we spent in researching, writing, and editing this book has not been as painful for them as many writers of books allege on behalf of their spouses.

Finally, our greatest thanks go to the fishermen and supporters of the industry who were our teachers and collaborators along the lake: "Darby" Barrington, Mr. and Mrs. Bob Bodi, Eric Bohl, Larry Davis, Ray Full, Jose Goncalves, Emma Gowitzka, Luther Gowitzka, Tom Gowitzka, Don Hallock, Joe Herr, Bob Higgins, Percy Holl, Jerry Hosko, Mr. and Mrs. Martin Hosko, Mr. and Mrs. Chester Jackson, Chuck Kaman, Mr. and Mrs. Lewis Keller, Lester Kishman, Dean Koch, Paul Leidorf, Tim Longnecker, Jerry Neidler, Mel Randall, William Resor, Frank Reynolds, Tony Santos, Roy Shepherd, Donald Smith, Alva Snell, Henry Snyder, Frank Turinsky, Jim Van Hoose, John Verissimo, Mr. and Mrs. Kenny Wahl, George Wakefield, "Whitey," and Marcus Zimmerman. We hope this book meets with their approval and is of use to them.

Preface: Fieldwork Methods and Analytic Approaches

Lake Erie is divided into three basins: the Western, containing about fifteen percent of the lake's area, which runs from Toledo to Cedar Point, just east of Sandusky; the Central, containing about sixty percent of the lake's area, which runs to Presque Isle, Pennsylvania; and the Eastern, containing about twenty-five percent of the lake's area, which runs to Buffalo. Our fieldwork was carried out in the area between Toledo and Vermilion—in the Western Basin and the westernmost part of the Central Basin (fig. 1).

We began our fieldwork along the western Lake Erie shore in March 1983 and ended our work in September 1985. During that time, we observed and photographed active fishermen at work—on trap-net and gill-net boats, at seining sites and in fish houses—and retired fishermen at their homes or habitual gathering and talking places (figs. 2–15). We recorded interviews with active and retired fishermen, and in some cases with their wives, both at work and at leisure. We photographed boats, nets, and other items of equipment and made copies of photographs in the collections of local fishermen and of the Great Lakes Historical Society in Vermilion, Ohio.

We began the initial interviews by asking questions about the current and past practices of the occupation, and in so doing directly presented ourselves as teachers and writers from the university in Columbus who wanted to write a book on commercial fishing that would present the occupation from the fishermen's point of view and largely in their own words. The idea of the "fishermen's point of view" seemed to stimulate some fishermen to discuss the political and economic situation of the entire occupation; in other cases, especially with older or retired fishermen, the idea was taken as a stimulus for more personal recollections. In most cases, particularly in the course of repeated interviews, both senses of the idea seemed to govern their conversations with us. We were open to whatever kind of traditional lore we might encounter and were actively seeking folk beliefs, weather signs, proverbs, legends, and jokes. However, these kinds of folklore were not forthcoming; instead, the fishermen usually talked about their own experiences, and we shifted our attention to these personal experience narratives.

Over the course of our fieldwork we began to notice certain recurring themes in conversations and narratives (some of which led to the organization of this book); as fieldworkers do, we began to try to direct our conversations toward these themes, while still trying to maintain an open-ended situation. Our field notes and interview transcripts clearly reveal this double tendency. The themes we discerned (often called *etic* in the scholarship) are based on our perceptions as folklorists, but we feel that they are similar to native distinctions (*emic*) fishermen would make (Dundes 1962; Pike 1954–60). Each individual fisherman saw his occupation from his own point of view, which was itself influenced by group concerns. We have tried to present those individual and group concerns within an overview based on our scholarly perspective. In the final analysis, the categories of narrative are ours, but they are based on a careful examination of all the material the fishermen presented to us. We feel that in the course of the interviews, a mutual trust developed between folklorist and fisherman: we trusted them to honestly present their occupation, and they trusted us to accurately represent their views to the public.

Our fieldwork was conducted during many trips, ranging in length from a few days to a month and made both individually and together. We tried to follow a plan that would allow us to cover all areas of the western lake (Toledo to Vermilion) and all parts of the occupation (trap netting, gill netting, seining, and fish house work), and to interview fishermen at all chronological stages (beginning, active, and retired) and levels of work (crew members, crew leaders, net work specialists, fishing boat owners, and fish house laborers and operators). We were fairly successful in this effort, except in the case of active gill netters, many of whom (particularly the many Portuguese who fished this technique) left the area when gill netting was prohibited, before we had had much chance to talk with them. We tried when possible to interview two or more fishermen at once. In these situations we

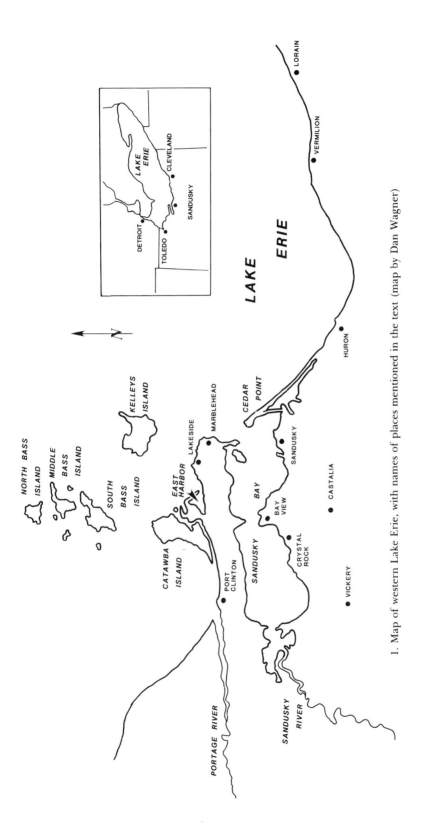

1. Map of western Lake Erie, with names of places mentioned in the text (map by Dan Wagner)

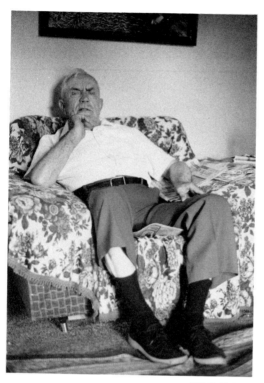

2. Luther Gowitzka, Castalia
(photo by Patrick Mullen)

3. Don Hallock, Sandusky
(photo by PM)

4. Joe Herr (*left*), Curtice, and Paul Leidorf, Port Clinton (photo by PM)

5. Jerry Hosko, Port Clinton (photo by PM)

6. Mr. and Mrs. Martin Hosko, Oregon, Ohio (photo by PM)

7. Lewis Keller, Marblehead (photo by PM)

8. Dean Koch, Castalia, piloting his trap-net boat off Sandusky (photo by PM)

9. Alva Snell, Vermilion (photo by PM)

10. John Verissimo, Vermilion, refinishing his gill-net tug (photo by PM)

11. Mr. and Mrs. Bob Bodi, Toledo (photo by PM)

12. Percy Holl (*left*) and Chester Jackson, Vermilion (photo by PM)

13. Chester Jackson with dip net and fishermen's lunch bucket (photo by PM)

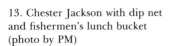

14. Marcus Zimmerman, Huron
(photo by PM)

15. Dean Koch's seining crew: *left to right*, Thomas Gowitzka, Sandusky;
Timothy Longnecker, Vickery; Donald Smith, Sandusky; Henry Snyder, Vickery
(photo by Timothy Lloyd)

could take the sort of background role we preferred to take and simply let fishermen talk with one another, although our presence remained an element of the situation. This was particularly helpful in those cases where the group of fishermen included men from different levels of the occupation (crew members and a crew leader or boat owner, for instance); it made different roles and points of view clearer.

We formally interviewed a total of twenty-seven people (fishermen, their wives, fish house owners and workers, and others knowledgeable about fishing) and talked to another eight fishermen who were working at the time and unable to be interviewed. We used quoted material from eighteen of the thirty-five people contacted. As mentioned above, we interviewed some fishermen's wives, although because so much of our work was centered in the workplace and because no women (except those working in the retail side of the fish house operations) are directly involved in the occupation in the area, we did not pursue this as much as we should have. When the opportunity arose, however, we did directly ask for wives' points of view.

We shot about seven hundred slides and almost eleven hundred black-and-white photographs in the course of our work, the subjects of which can be grouped into five major categories: the three fishing techniques, fish house activities, boats and equipment, nets and net work, and portraits of the fishermen with whom we worked. All of the slides and approximately ninety percent of the black-and-white photographs are of contemporary subjects; the remainder of the black-and-white photographs are copies of historical photographs from local collections. As in our interviews, we attempted to document the widest range of the occupation. On most of our joint trips, we shared the photographic responsibilities; one of us shot color, the other black-and-white. When we worked alone, we usually carried two cameras or camera bodies. Thus, with the exception of the historical photographs, the slides and prints document the same subjects, activities, and events. Copies of our contact sheets and slides, with indexes, have been given to the Center for Lake Erie Area Research at the Ohio State University in Columbus and to the Great Lakes Historical Society in Vermilion for their archives. The original slides, negatives, and contact sheets, as well as the tapes, indexes, and transcripts of our interviews, are on file at the Ohio Arts Council in Columbus, where they can be examined upon request.

As we completed fieldwork trips, we indexed our photographic materials and interview tapes. At the conclusion of our fieldwork, we had all of our tapes transcribed. The next six months were taken up with reading and review of the transcripts and with extended discussions of ways to organize the materials for this book. Our major alternatives seemed to be organizing the book in terms of individual fishermen and their narratives of all sorts, organizing it in terms of narrative topics with contributions in each section from many fishermen, or organizing it by some combination of these two principles. We chose the second alternative, as we judged it more important to place the recurring themes in fishermen's occupational narratives, and the ways in which those narratives embody the occupational identity of those who tell them, in the foreground. Luckily, we have also been able to include a good deal of individual biography within this scheme.

Like any local industry, the commercial fishery of western Lake Erie is greatly affected by the regional, national, and world economies of which it is a part. Although a complete understanding of the economic realities of the local occupation would include consideration of these wider contexts of fish harvesting, distribution, and consumption, we have drawn the boundaries of the present study to delimit a smaller world. We have chosen to concentrate on specific expressions of local people about local circumstances, in some part because it is with individual conversational expression that folklore work often begins, and in some part because of the relative lack of attention paid to individual expression in the existing work on fishing cultures. Our study is not a complete ethnography or socioeconomic work; rather, it is a presentation and analysis of a body of local knowledge that should complement the other, broader studies that are or will be available.

The principles for selecting excerpts from the complete transcripts were relevance to the focus of the study, accurate representation of group values and beliefs, skill in storytelling, and entertainment value for the reader. We have tried to include entire statements without deletions, but in a few instances repetitious material, digressions, and parts of the recording that could not be transcribed have been deleted. All three kinds of deletions have been indicated by ellipses (. . .). When our questions seemed to direct an answer, we have included the question in the quoted material. Once the selections were made, we then individually wrote separate parts of the manuscript, reviewed and criticized each other's work, and revised the entire manuscript for submission, checking each other's production along the way.

The heart of the book is made up of the fishermen telling their own stories in their own words with some description of the contexts by the authors. The narratives are presented within the framework of the thematic and analytic focus of each particular chapter. For instance, chapter 2 focuses on the past, and as the analytic frame we use the ways in which retired fishermen's lives have shaped their view of the past. Our interpretation of the overall meaning of these stories is contained in the conclusion, Personal Narratives and Occupational Identity. The analysis is based on the scholarship of identity, which is cross-disciplinary and includes work from anthropology, folklore, social psychology, psychoanalysis, ethnic studies, and education. Personal and social identity is revealed through the close scrutiny of individual narratives and conversations about occupational life.

From social psychology, the oppositional theory of Edward Spicer (1971) and the multiple identity theory of Marisa Zavalloni (1973, 1983) have direct and fruitful application to the folkloric study of occupational identity. There is a long and rich tradition of American folklore scholarship on occupations such as cowboys, miners, oilfield workers, and railroaders (Lomax 1910; Green 1972; Korson 1938; Boatright 1963; Botkin and Harlow 1953), but these works have concentrated on established genres of folklore including ballads, legends, folk beliefs, and tall tales. More recent occupational scholarship has begun to explore personal experience narratives (Byington 1978; Curry 1983; Harper 1987; Ives 1978; McCarl 1985; Santino 1983). A valuable cross-cultural context for the study of the narratives of Lake Erie fishermen is provided by the extensive scholarship on the anthropology of fishing cultures (see Acheson 1981; Landberg 1973, 1979; Orbach and Harper 1979). Several works have concentrated on the North Atlantic in both North America and England (Andersen 1979; Andersen and Wadel 1972; Faris 1972; Forrest 1988; Fricke 1973; Poggie and Gersuny 1974; Thompson, Wailey, and Lummis 1985; Tunstall 1962). Other studies have been conducted throughout the western world on both deep sea and bay and lake fishing (Gunda 1984; Hasslof, Henningsen, and Christiansen 1972; Matthiessen 1986; Orbach 1977; Smith 1977; Warner 1976). A number of local studies have focused on fishermen's narratives about their work (Butcher 1980; Chowning 1983; Clifford 1974; Green 1985; Thompson 1950; Van Winkle 1975; Wilbur and Wentworth 1986). Folklorists have also been active in studying maritime cultures (Gilmore 1986; Johnson

1988; Lund 1983; Mullen 1978b). Although the concept of identity has been included in these studies, the dual focus on identity and personal experience narratives has not been a part of maritime studies scholarship until now. Personal narratives reveal the complex intertwining of individual and social identity in ways that no other verbal expressions can.

Personal narratives are an important part of any group's folklore, a fact long recognized in folklore scholarship (Bausinger 1958; Jolles 1965; Neumann 1967; Sydow 1948). A renewed interest in personal narrative came about in the United States in the 1970s as folklorists came to realize that changing circumstances in society were causing folklore forms to evolve. In this regard Linda Degh has pointed out: "As folklorists leave behind the old confines of traditional society and pursue folk narrative as it steps out of the straitjacket of genre categories, they realize how narration can be an immediate reflection of culture. Modern life changes the picture all around; folklorists scrutinize new sources and new processes such as the reduction, replacement, and the reinforcement of old forms" (1972, 78). In her topics of "everyday stories," Degh includes labor reminiscences and autobiographical stories, two categories that apply to the narratives of commercial fishermen (1972, 79). Several factors help define the personal experience narrative as folklore: tradition, recurring performance, and self-contained unity. Personal stories are traditional in style of presentation, in the values, beliefs, and symbols being projected, and in the context of performance. "No matter how loose the structure and how flexible the framework of these everyday stories, they follow the trend of the more established genres. They use such devices as threefold repetition, dramatized dialogues, and endings signaled with a bang" (Degh 1972, 78).

Even if a story is based on something that happened to the teller and to no one else, it will still reflect traditional community concerns; the teller will select what he or she and the culture determine is significant to narrate and will tell it in a manner and at a place and time considered appropriate. If a story is told only once, it may not have met all of the cultural criteria for a significant narrative; recurring performance is a factor in determining traditionality (Abrahams 1976, 195). The narrative also has a conventional structure; it has a beginning, middle, and end; it will be set apart from conversation as a self-contained unit of communication (Abrahams 1972, 18; Babcock 1984,

66–67, 71; Toelken 1979, 32). In our study, we use Barbara Herrnstein Smith's succinct definition of narrative as "verbal acts consisting of *someone telling someone else that something happened*" (1980, 232; also see Labov 1972). In the conversational situation in which the story is told, the listeners recognize the expression as a story separate from the surrounding communication (Robinson 1981; Stahl 1977b).

Most of the stories included in this book fit the criteria given above: fishermen's personal narratives are self-contained units and most are performed repeatedly; they all contain and reflect traditional values and attitudes of the individual and group. Some of the fishermen were better storytellers than others, and the narratives of the good storytellers were more likely to have recurring performances. A few stories were given only because of the interview situation and were not told often otherwise. These may not be as aesthetically pleasing, but they are just as valuable as social documents and as expressions of identity. As part of our study, we have also included non-narrative material: statements in conversation made separately from stories, which express some of the same concerns that the narratives do. These statements are taken with other cultural and social information as context to better understand and interpret the narratives themselves. The personal experience narratives of commercial fishermen on western Lake Erie are a significant element in their traditional lives, and they provide a revealing example of how occupational and individual identities are determined by complex social, cultural, and individual forces.

Lake Erie Fishermen

Introduction: Commercial Fishing on Lake Erie

A. The Current State of the Occupation

Early most mornings between March and October, the hundred or so commercial fishermen working on the Ohio waters of western Lake Erie leave home for fish houses, boat docks, and seining sites between Toledo and Vermilion. At three or four o'clock in the afternoon, they head home for supper after a day's work that is likely to have netted them fewer fish for market than did the same day a year before. Contrary to popular belief, Lake Erie is not biologically "dead," nor was it ever as sterile as it was widely reported to have become. Economic as well as biological changes, especially those that mark the shift of government and business support from commercial fishing to sport fishing, are responsible for the shorter season, smaller and less-profitable catches, and general hard times of commercial fishermen in the area.

As the name implies, commercial fishing is a business, the procedure of which is to trade fuel, equipment, and human effort (which all cost money) for fish (which bring money). The techniques of commercial fishing—designing, making, and repairing boats, nets, and other equipment; knowing how, when, and where to find fish of certain species; dividing labor on the boat; *setting, lifting,* and *pulling* nets (placing nets in the water, taking fish from them, and removing nets from the water, respectively); predicting weather conditions and handling close calls with storms and other traffic on the lake; outwitting the authorities by bending or breaking regulations; and so on—all have to do with minimizing the amount of expense and effort needed to catch the maximum tonnage of fish.

Over the past century, many technological innovations have made fishermen's work more efficient, both on Lake Erie and elsewhere. Fishermen now use boats made more stoutly of steel instead of wood and powered more reliably by gasoline instead of wind or steam. They now use improved weather reporting and sometimes specialized fish-finding equipment to supplement their own skills. More important, they now use nets made of synthetic materials, which last longer than those of twine.

Nevertheless, for these techniques and innovations to have been incorporated into the occupation they must have been fitted into the system of human experience and skill shared by fishermen as a group. Whatever the economics or equipment may be, inexperienced fishermen learn the occupation informally from experienced fishermen in the course of day-to-day, trial and error participation in the work itself. Knowing what to do in a particular situation and how to do it makes one a functioning part of the group. What makes fishermen fishermen is this shared body of knowledge, passed on through work and away from work in narratives that express the group's occupational identity.

Not everything that commercial fishermen say is in narrative form or is related to fishing, of course, and a good part of their oral communication is tied up with basic on-the-job instructions (in which occupational jargon plays a great part) or with conversational topics shared with the population at large; for example, current happenings, domestic life, sports, politics, and the like. Much of their talk, though, does have narrative structure and a specific connection to the occupation. In the chapters that follow, we have organized both brief and lengthy excerpts (narrative and non-narrative) from tape-recorded interviews with active and retired commercial fishermen (and, in some cases, with their wives) into categories based upon recurring themes in our conversations with fishermen: techniques and customs of the occupation, the past, notable local fishermen, hazards of work on the lake, the importance and value of the occupation to those who practice it, and the conflicts they have with outsiders, particularly sport fishermen and enforcement wardens with whom commercial fishermen share the lake.

Conflict is an important issue to Ohio commercial fishermen. They work under a large number of regulations, conceived and written by the Division of Wildlife of the Ohio Department of Natural Resources and partly codified by the state legislature, the Ohio General Assembly. There are regulations on the length of the fishing season for each of the two remaining fishing techniques; on the possibility (basically, none) of obtaining a new commercial fishing license or of transferring an existing license to another individual; on areas of the lake that may be fished commercially, either at all or at certain times of the season; on the total length or number of nets per license; on the maximum dimensions of nets and their minimum *mesh* size (a mesh, measured in linear inches, is the size of the "holes" in a net; fishermen speak of a "two-inch" or a "four-inch" mesh); on the proper identification of nets; on the times of day when fishing is allowed; on the species that can legally be taken from the lake; on the minimum size of legal fish species that can be taken; and on other aspects of the industry. These regulations change from time to time, of course, in response to changes in the lake ecosystem documented and analyzed by biologists or, as fishermen often allege, in response to more or less direct political pressure from sport fishing or other related interests, which commercial fishermen believe to be allied against them. These regulations are enforced through the detailed records that fishermen and fish house operators are required to maintain and submit and, more directly, through unannounced spot checks of any part of a fishing operation by Ohio Division of Wildlife enforcement officers, who are empowered to confiscate illegal catches and to cite fishermen or fish house operators for the violation of regulations.

To commercial fishermen in the area, the most crucial short-term regulations are those concerning mesh size, because an increase in the minimum size means that entire net stocks become instantly useless and must be replaced at high cost, and those concerning fish size limits, because an increase in the minimum legal size for one or more species can mean more wasted time and effort throwing back undersized fish and can also make existing nets obsolete. The most problematic long-term regulations are those concerning legal species. Over the past twenty-five years—especially since the Lake Erie "mercury scare" (as fishermen call it) of 1970, when commercial fishing on Lake Erie and other Great Lakes was temporarily banned because of an increase of mercury levels in lake fish—the variety of species that Ohio fishermen can legally take has been much curtailed. A major loss occurred in

1972, when Ohio commercial fishermen were prohibited from taking *walleye*, the most popular sport fish in the lake, usually sold under the name of "pickerel" at fish markets and seafood restaurants along the lake and throughout the region. It is particularly irksome to Ohio commercial fishermen that the pickerel on restaurant tables in their state must be imported (at higher cost) from Canada, on whose side of the lake the fish can be commercially taken. "I never saw a line drawn on the lake," said more than one fisherman. Whatever side of this controversy you support, it is clear that commercial fishermen have been left with fewer species to take, many of which are less desirable for human consumption and thus have a lower wholesale value: sheephead, gizzard shad, buffalo, suckers, carp, white perch, and the like, what fishermen call *trash fish.*

Over the past two decades, sport fishing has grown to be a substantial business along the lake. To be more correct, it is a group of businesses, evidenced by the increasing numbers of marinas, hotels, restaurants, and summertime condominium developments along the shoreline. The economic value of sport fishing is considerable, and the sport fishery is an economic complex that the State of Ohio does not want to jeopardize. Commercial fishermen argue that the lake is large and bountiful enough for all to share, but that the state government and those involved in the business of sport fishing (not so much the average hook-and-line fishermen, but the well-to-do sportsmen who own summer homes and large boats, as well as those who service them) regard fishing as a "zero-sum" situation, in which one side's gain must be the other's loss.

From the fishermen's point of view (and from ours as well), this situation rests partly on a conflict of images. Commercial fishermen in general are usually portrayed either as hardy individualists, working with (or against) nature in ways that those who do other kinds of work can only dimly imagine, or as poor, uneducated idlers and drinkers who contribute to the ill-being of the communities they inhabit. As Janet Gilmore, who has studied Oregon's commercial fisheries, has pointed out, the positive stereotype conforms to the image fishermen tend to hold of themselves (what has been called an esoteric image), and the second, negative stereotype conforms to the image many outsiders hold of fishermen (what has been called an exoteric image) (Jansen 1959). This negative stereotype also conforms to the image commercial fishermen, with some justification, believe others hold of them (Gilmore 1983).

Commercial fishermen regard themselves as self-educated and self-made as well as self-employed men. Their knowledge of the lake and the fish that inhabit it has been formed through daily exposure to the problems of making a living by harvesting (as they see it) the lake. They regard the lake's unpredictability as part of the nature of the territory; they have developed techniques to make the best of it, and they regard their occupational independence as an entitlement based upon their knowledge and skill. At the same time, it is an inescapable fact that many commercial fishermen are no longer as independent as they say they are or as they would prefer to be. Their work is greatly regulated, fewer young people want to (or can) enter the occupation, and many fishermen must take wage labor at manufacturing plants or other area businesses to supplement their income—work in which they are usually subject to the dictates of others or, as in assembly-line work, to the method of production itself.

Like any group of workers, fishermen do not appreciate what they see as interference from those whose knowledge, they feel, is based only upon "theory" removed from the test of day-to-day experience. They take considerable pride and glee in relating stories of enforcement agents who cannot tell one species of fish from another, of bureaucrats whose boats run out of gas in the middle of the lake and who must be rescued by passing commercial boats, and of their own skills in outwitting regulations and those who enforce them. Given the fishermen's point of view, it is neither surprising that they try to find ways to get around or ignore the rules nor unusual that they see themselves as guiltless, "Robin Hood" figures for doing so.

Because we conducted our fieldwork at a time when these conflicts were very much on the minds of local fishermen, and because we expressed an interest in learning about the occupation from the fishermen's point of view, many of our conversations with them dealt greatly with the subject, in both its negative and positive aspects. Fishermen complained about regulations and sport fishing and told stories about supposedly trumped-up arrests, and they asserted their own ideas about the value and importance of commercial fishing, in both an economic and personal sense. Had we conducted our work at an earlier time (say, the 1930s and 1940s, which both fishermen's recollections and published reports of the time reveal as good years, on the whole, for the occupation), we might have heard a different version. Or perhaps not; most workers, as Jack Santino has pointed out, speak of a departed "golden age" in their occupation, and fishermen forty or fifty years ago may have thought their own times hard, and those of the turn of the century better (1978, 204).

Our stance toward the political and economic problems of the fishermen is influenced by our contact with them, and we are obviously sympathetic to their plight. At the same time, we recognize the complexity of the situation; there are many matters of need to consider, including the need to protect the lake's environment, the need for economic growth in the towns along the shore, the concerns of sport fishermen, and the rights of commercial fishermen to pursue their occupation. We feel that all of these needs can be met through balanced legislation and regulations that consider all of the interested groups and the public welfare. To this point, however, the concerns of commercial fishermen have not been widely known. We see this book as an opportunity for them to tell their side of the story.

B. A Brief History of Lake Erie Commercial Fishing

Before the intensive European settlement of the Lake Erie area following the War of 1812, a Native American fishery existed on and around the lake (This section draws heavily on two sources: Applegate and Van Meter 1970; Barnes 1983). It was primarily a subsistence industry and used brush *weirs* (handmade fences set into streams for catching fish) and other simple fishing techniques. At the time, the temperature of the lake was lower than it is today, and a number of coldwater species—lake sturgeon, lake trout, northern pike, muskellunge, sauger, and blue pike, for example—existed in much greater numbers than today, along with typical warmwater species—white bass, channel catfish, black bass, crappies, and sunfish.

The first commercial fishing on Lake Erie was a hook-and-line fishery for muskellunge at Presque Isle begun at the time of first European settlement. A shore seine fishery in the Maumee River began around 1815, and by 1830 fishing had become an important local industry. Cotton twine replaced brush as the common netting material and was used in the construction of *seines, drag nets*, weirs, *trotlines*, spears, and lines for *hook-and-line* fishing. Mill dams were often constructed on tributaries to block the upstream passage of migrating fish so they could be caught. Most fishing at this time was done in rivers, bays, and marshes near shore and was confined mostly to the Ohio shore.

Around 1850 the *pound net* (the ancestor of today's trap net) was introduced in the Western Basin of Lake Erie, as were *gill nets* in the Eastern Basin. Both these types of gear made offshore deeper-water fishing, carried out by sailing vessels, a more feasible enterprise. By 1860, pound-net fishing had become predominant in the western part of the lake. An extensive trotline fishery, primarily for bullheads and channel catfish, also developed in Ohio waters during this period. These efficient fishing techniques, along with improved preservation methods (canning and freezing), more extensive and rapid rail transportation, and the increased demand for foodstuffs during the Civil War contributed to the development of a strong Lake Erie commercial fishery.

Unfortunately, the catch records for these years are few and incomplete. Annual commercial fish landings were not systematically recorded in the United States and Canada until the early 1870s, and even these were often sporadic and lacking in detail. Based on the available records for 1815–70, muskellunge, northern pike, largemouth and smallmouth bass, lake sturgeon, yellow perch, and white bass were among the first species to attain commercial importance, especially in the bay and river seine fisheries. Lake herring, lake whitefish, and lake trout then became important in the mid-1800s as pound and gill nets made offshore harvest of these species more efficient. Whitefish and herring became the most economically important commercial species in the lake in the late 1800s as pound- and gill-net fishing came to dominate the lake.

By the 1880s a geographical pattern in the use of fishing techniques had emerged that was to remain in place, with few modifications, until the prohibition of gill-net fishing in all Ohio Lake Erie waters in 1984: a predominance of gill-net fishing in the Central and (after 1920) the Eastern Basins, and of pound-net, *fyke net*, and *trap net* fishing in the Western Basin. As the western part of the lake warmed, gill nets were used for the larger coldwater species—lake trout, lake whitefish, lake sturgeon, sauger, and blue pike—in the east, and the other, related net types for warmwater species—lake herring, walleye, yellow perch, and channel catfish—in the west. Although the Ohio commercial fishery, centered in Sandusky, was preeminent during this period, the

Canadian pound-net fishery, which had previously lagged far behind that of the United States, began a significant increase after 1880, concentrating on the catching of lake herring.

In response to overexploitation and changing environmental conditions, the population of important species of fish began to decline during the last quarter of the nineteenth century. Lake herring and lake whitefish, which had supported an intensive, high-value, and high-profit commercial fishery, began to decline in the late 1800s, and lower value "coarse" fish—sauger, walleye, yellow perch, blue pike, channel catfish, and white bass—increased in commercial importance. Decreases in herring and whitefish catches led to the first attempts at governmental regulation and management of the Lake Erie fisheries. State and provincial governments proposed set fishing seasons and artificial propagation and stocking schemes. These attempts were complicated and often made impotent by the division of the lake among Ontario, New York, Pennsylvania, Ohio, and Michigan jurisdictions and by chronic disagreements over regulatory and management strategies—problems that remain to this day.

Steam-powered fishing vessels came increasingly into use on the lake after 1900, and the introduction of the steam gill-net lifter made gill nets even more efficient to use. Gill netting then moved back into importance in the Eastern Basin. Steam power subsequently gave way to gasoline and diesel power in the fishing fleet. Because of the increasing efficiency of both gill and trap nets, pound nets were no longer used to any significant extent after the mid-1930s.

Good commercial fishery statistics were available on a regular basis after 1900. Fish landings throughout the lake declined steadily during the 1920s largely due to the collapse of the lake herring fishery around 1925. Commercial landings of important coldwater species, especially northern pike and muskellunge, also declined; after 1915, these species were no longer significant.

By 1930, commercial fishing methods in the lake were much like the present. Gill netting prevailed throughout Canadian waters and in the United States waters of the Eastern and Central Basins. Trap netting and shore *seining* dominated in the United States Western Basin. Seining was largely confined, as it is today, to the Sandusky and Maumee Bays and to the shallow nearshore waters west of Port Clinton. Commercial fish landings throughout the lake levelled off during this period, with no new losses of species to the fishery. However, species that had already begun to decline, especially coldwater and coolwater species, continued to do so as the lake continued to warm, an effect of increased population and industrial activity. Declines in the abundance of lake herring and lake whitefish were offset, to some extent, by increased landings of walleye and white bass, which were becoming more popular fish for human consumption. The 1930s marked the end of high-profit fisheries based upon coldwater species. However, the great demand for inexpensive protein of all kinds generated by the depression and World War II still supported some coldwater fishing despite its lower profit.

Two major changes in fishing technology occurred in Lake Erie during the 1950s. Nylon nets, which could be fished continuously and were two to three times as efficient as twine nets, came into extensive use. *Trawling* for rainbow smelt was introduced experimentally in Ohio and Pennsylvania waters in 1958; although it was never adopted there, it became a major operation in Canadian waters, eventually accounting for the bulk of the yearly Canadian catch by weight.

In the early 1950s, a period of great instability in the Lake Erie fisheries began. Although commercial fish landings increased during the 1950s, they did so mostly because of the use of nylon nets, increased fishing effort lakewide, and the large catches in the Canadian smelt industry. During the 1950s, in fact, Canadian landings surpassed those of the United States for the first time, as the species on which the United States fishery depended declined and in some cases collapsed. By the 1960s, the composition of commercial fish landings from the lake had changed considerably. Canadian fisheries depended almost entirely on the intensive, government-subsidized harvest of yellow perch, walleye, and rainbow smelt, while United States fisheries depended on walleye and yellow perch as the main cash species, with other income from lower value species: channel catfish, white bass, carp, suckers, and freshwater drum. Although the stocks of these lower value species were abundant, the amounts landed were variable and subject to great fluctuations in seasonal demand.

In April 1970 all Ohio commercial fishing in Lake Erie was temporarily banned because of research that suggested a higher-than-acceptable level of mercury in lake fish. When commercial fishing resumed the following year, it did so under a number of new regulations, the most damaging of which was the prohibition against commercial fishing for walleye, one of the most important cash species of the industry. During the 1970s, an even greater percentage of commercial fishing income had to be derived from the lower value species mentioned above. In 1984, gill-net fishing in Ohio, which had previously been limited by regulation to the Eastern and Central Basins, was prohibited throughout the Ohio lake.

In summary, the development of Lake Erie commercial fishing over the past 175 years can be characterized in four ways. First among these is the increasing temperature of most of the lake and the eventual loss, because of this increase and because of overfishing, of many valuable coldwater and coolwater species. Second is the change, similar to those that have occurred in agriculture during the same period, from many commercial species to a few, most of which (at least for American fishermen) have lower value. Third is the technological improvement of fishing equipment and techniques, and fourth is increased government regulation, complicated by conflicting jurisdictions and policies. As we will see, this formal history parallels local fishermen's more personal and more critical narratives of a decline from a "golden age" they have experienced or heard about to the present difficulties of the occupation, especially in Ohio waters (Santino 1978, 204).

1

~~~~~~~~

Technique and Custom

Like all people with a common occupation, western Lake Erie fishermen recognize their fellow workers by a shared knowledge of work technique. The process of becoming a fisherman is the process of learning the fisherman's work through day-to-day, trial-and-error experience. It is accomplished by following orders, by practicing actions demonstrated by others, by referring to accepted ways of doing everyday work as they have been explained by more experienced fishermen, and by improvising solutions to new problems if traditional ways fall short. While this common knowledge is necessary for successful work to be done, it goes beyond matters of practical fishing procedure. It also has an evaluative and aesthetic side, through which the quality of work can be judged and the pleasure in cooperation and good work can be expressed. Bob Bodi and Martin Hosko, who worked together for many years out of Toledo, recalled their subtle cooperation.

> **BB:** We got to know each other so good that Martin didn't have to tell me what he was going to do. I knew what he was going to do, and he knew what I was going to do.
> **MH:** I make a little motion, and he knew what that motion meant. Just a little nudge with the hand, and he knew exactly what to do. Thank you, Bob.

In this chapter, we describe the work processes of the three types of fishing done in western Lake Erie, based on our observation of and our interviews with fishermen, and then examine the ways fishermen describe their knowledge of work techniques and customs as part of their occupational culture and identity.

During the time of our fieldwork, commercial fishermen used one of three specific fishing techniques in the Ohio waters of Lake Erie— trap netting, gill netting, and shore seining. Trap netting has been dominant in the western part of the lake for over a century. Gill netting was important in the eastern part of the area in which we worked and dominant farther east in the lake, until it was prohibited throughout the Ohio lake in 1984. Many former gillnetters now fish with deepwater trap nets in the Central Basin. Although seining has been a secondary technique for some time in the area, it has been carried on in the shallows of the western lake and its tributary bays since white settlement of the area began some 175 years ago.

Trap netting requires an elaborate and carefully designed net structure set in the water at a right angle to the suspected path of traveling fish (figs. 16–18). When fish confront the long *lead* of a trap net across their path, made of heavy-duty, tarred netting so that it can be seen by fish and so it can stay underwater for long periods of time, they turn and swim along it, through a funnel-shaped opening into a box of net (called a *crib*) inside which they are trapped alive. This type of fishing is done both close in and out away from shore, and the length and shape of the lead, the shape and size of the crib opening, the dimensions of the crib, and the placement of the nets vary depending upon the time of year, the intended location of the net, and the behavior of the species fished. Trap nets are marked in the water by *buoys* at the far end of the lead, at the *wings* (secondary leads that direct the fish toward the funnel and crib), and at the crib, all topped by flags with the fishing license-holder's name (fig. 19).

Upon arriving at the crib, the fishermen, using a powered winch, lift the crib up to the side of their boat; pass the fish into the boat with a small *dip net;* sort and size the fish, throwing back those that are too small or of illegal species; place the fish in plastic boxes by species; and ice them down for the trip back to the *fish house* (a wholesale/retail operation on shore) (figs. 20–30). Trap nets are set in the water for up to two weeks' time, depending upon weather and water conditions and fish movements. A typical trap-netting trip begins at six or seven o'clock in the morning, lasts until two or three o'clock in the afternoon, and can involve the lifting of eight to fifteen nets.

The trap-net boat differs in design from boats used in other types of commercial fishing (figs. 31–44). Approximately forty feet long, it has a small open cabin at the bow, below and just ahead of the wheel,

16-18. A finished trap net opened up inside a Kishman Fish Company shed in Vermilion, from the open end of the net structure (original photos courtesy of Ray Full, Kishman Fish Company)

17.

18.

19. A trap-net buoy, with lead
weights and flag identifying the
net's owner (photo by TL)

20. Trap-net fishermen eating by the winch (known locally as a "niggerhead") used to haul in the trap net. The *Gerald H.* was one of Martin Hosko's boats, named after his son Jerry (original photo courtesy of the *Toledo Blade* and Jerry Hosko, Jerry's Bait Company, Port Clinton)

21. Dean Koch's trap-net boat begins the lifting of a trap net, as the first part of the net is winched on board. The crew on the two occasions photographed included Don Hallock, Bob Higgins, Thomas Gowitzka, Timothy Longnecker, and Jerry Neidler (photo by PM)

22. Removing fish caught in other parts of the net (photo by PM)

23. Pulling in more of the net crib (photo by PM)

24. Dip-netting fish out of the crib (photo by PM)

25. Don Hallock passes fish to Dean Koch for sorting and culling (photo by PM)

26. Dean Koch sorts perch. Note the minimum length marks for different species scratched into the box (photo by PM)

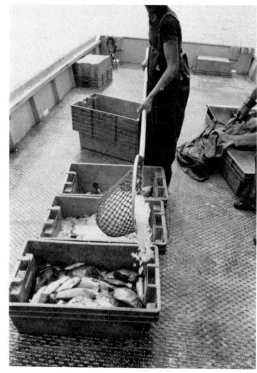

27. Once fish are sorted and culled, they are iced for the trip to shore (photo by PM)

28. Trap netters at work in the 1950s (original photo courtesy of the *Toledo Blade* and Jerry Hosko)

29. Wooden boxes of the sort once used to carry caught fish, now replaced by plastic ones (photo by TL)

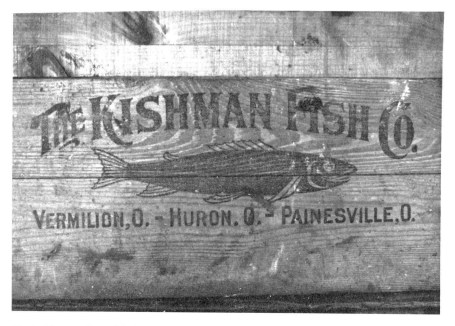

30. A shipment box with the Kishman Fish Company's logo (photo by TL)

31. The trap-net boat *Ray F.* docked at Kishman Fish Company, Vermilion, showing the bow cabin, wheel, "niggerhead," and anchors stacked on the deck. Ray Full, after whom the boat is named, was the long-time manager of Kishman Fish until his recent death (photo by TL)

32. The "niggerhead," wheel, and gearbox of another Kishman trap-net boat (photo by TL)

33. The wheel and instrument panel of the *Ray F.* (photo by TL)

34. A small St. Christopher medal above the windshield of the *Ray F.* (photo by TL)

35-38. Historical photographs of trap-net boats returning to port with the bumper loads of fish common twenty or thirty years ago (original photos 35 and 36 courtesy of Jerry Hosko and the *Toledo Blade*, which customarily used such photos to illustrate yearly stories about the season's first catch. Original photos 37 and 38 courtesy of Alva Snell, Vermilion)

36.

37.

38.

39. Historical photograph of early trap-net boats leaving Huron in 1912 (original photo courtesy of Alva Snell)

40. Trap-net boats leaving Cleveland in the 1950s (original photo courtesy of the Great Lakes Historical Society, Vermilion)

41. The *Florence H.*, one of Martin Hosko's early trap-net boats, built in 1938 (original photo courtesy of Jerry Hosko)

42. Lifting a pound net (the ancestor of the trap net) into a Lay Brothers sail-powered boat, about 1910 (original photo courtesy of the Great Lakes Historical Society)

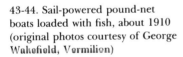

43-44. Sail-powered pound-net boats loaded with fish, about 1910 (original photos courtesy of George Wakefield, Vermilion)

44.

45. Gill-netter John Verissimo
setting up netting for repair
in his basement shop
(photo by PM)

46-47. John Verissimo at work on
his nets (photos by PM)

47.

48. A fisherman working on a gill
net in the 1930s (original photo
courtesy of the Great Lakes
Historical Society.)

49. Scraps of gill net drying on racks at the Kishman Fish Company yard (photo by TL)

50. The bow pulley on John Verissimo's gill-net tug, beginning to haul in a line of gill nets (photo by PM)

51. As the gill net enters the bow of the tug, it is stacked for later sorting and culling of fish (photo by PM)

52-55. Extracting the fish from the gill net, a job that must be done fish by fish, and by hand. The crew includes Tony Santos, Chuck Kaman, Jose Goncalves, William Resor, and Eric Bohl (photos by PM)

53.

54.

55.

56. Guiding the gill net back into the water from the stern after the fish have been removed (photo by PM)

57. Cleaning the inside of the tug on the way back to the fish house (photo by PM)

58. The gill-net tug *Roberta* tied up at Kishman Fish Company in Vermilion (photo by TL)

59. Historical photograph of a gill-net tug tied up at Kishman Fish. Note the racks for drying gill nets behind the tug, which are the same as those shown in disrepair years later in figure 49 (original photo courtesy of Ray Full)

60. A 1915 photo of the Kishman tug *Edward K.*, the last steam-powered gill-net tug, in for repairs (original photo courtesy of Ray Full)

61. A Kishman gill-net tug from the early years of this century (photo courtesy Alva Snell)

62. Dean Koch's seine net, piled on a skiff from the previous day's work and ready to be set in Sandusky Bay off Crystal Rock (photo by TL)

63. Hauling out the seine net (photo by TL)

64. The half-mile-long net, with quarter-mile lines at each end, plays out into the bay (photo by TL)

65. The seiner's shack at Crystal Rock. The winch for bringing in the seine sits under the porch roof (photo by TL)

66. The winch. Note its two arms, similar to the "niggerhead" on a trap-net boat, which bring in the lines at the ends of the seine (photo by PM)

67. The net begins to come in. Note the floats on the top line of the net; the bottom line is weighted (photo by TL)

68. Staking up the bag in which the fish are caught (photo by TL)

69. The bag, full of fish (photo by TL)

70. Culling fish from the bag (photo by TL)

71. Some of the stakes used to fix
the bag in place (photo by PM)

72. The skiffs used to sort and cull fish (photo by TL)

73. The dip net used to pass fish from the bag into the skiff (photo by PM)

74. A June 1951 *Toledo Blade* Sunday Supplement article on Lake Erie seining (courtesy of Kenny Wahl, Sandusky)

75. Fishermen sorting and culling fish from a seine in the 1940s (original photo courtesy of Ray Full)

76-79. Part of a sequence of photographs mounted on the wall at the Port Clinton Fish Company showing a seine pull in bad weather from the 1960s (original photos courtesy of Jim Van Hoose, Port Clinton Fish Company)

77.

78.

79.

80. The main building at the Kishman Fish Company, at the mouth of the Vermilion River in downtown Vermilion (photo by TL)

81. Sign announcing the development of vacation condominiums on the Kishman Fish Company site (photo by PM)

82. Conveyor belt at Kishman Fish, used for transporting fish from boats into the building for processing (photo by TL)

83. Conveyor belt at Port Clinton Fish Company, bringing in a trap-net catch (photo by TL)

84. Weighing fish just before icing and shipment at Port Clinton Fish Company (photo by TL)

85. One of the Kishman Fish Company's fleet of refrigerator trucks (photo by TL)

86. Packing fish at the Lay Brothers Fishery, about 1910 (original photo courtesy of the Great Lakes Historical Society)

87-97. Men at work at Martin Hosko's fish house during the 1950s. Photographs of local fishing operations during this time, especially those taken by newspaper photographers, emphasize the abundance of the commercial fishery (original photos courtesy of the *Toledo Blade* and Jerry Hosko)

88.

89.

90.

91.

92.

93.

94.

95.

96.

97.

98. Dean Koch's trap-net crew members (*left to right:* Don Hallock, Jerry Neidler, Thomas Gowitzka, and Timothy Longnecker) relax and talk on the way back to Shoreline Fish Company in Sandusky after a trap-netting trip (photo by PM)

99. Two trap nets laid out after repair and retarring in Dean Koch's net yard in Crystal Rock (photo by PM)

100. Don Hallock, Dean Koch's main net man, repairing trap nets (photo by PM)

101. Detail of Don Hallock at work (photo by PM)

102. The "needle" used to hold repair twine and reknot damaged sections of net (photo by PM)

103. The equipment used to heat tar for net restoration (photo by TL)

104-6. Historical photographs of men at work in a net yard. Figures 105 and 106 show the tarring of nets (original photos courtesy of Jerry Hosko)

105.

106.

and low sides for ease in lifting and pulling nets out of the water. The deck is wide and flat to accommodate the boxes of fish for the trip back to the fish house. Steel boats replaced wooden ones about sixty years ago. There once were a number of individual boatbuilders and boatbuilding companies along the Ohio shore of the western lake, but today there is only one metal-fabricating firm equipped to build commercial fishing boats. In recent years, this company has only repaired boats for those fishermen who could not make their own repairs, because the fishing business is no longer lucrative enough to justify the expense of $20,000 for a new boat.

When we began our fieldwork, gill netting was limited by state regulation to those sections of the Ohio lake east of the Vermilion River mouth, and the only three remaining gill-net ports were Vermilion, Cleveland, and, just west of the Ohio-Pennsylvania border, Conneaut (the last two of this group lay outside the area in which we worked). In 1984, however, gill netting was prohibited in all Ohio waters of the lake. A single gill net is roughly six feet high and fifty feet long, although a number of nets may be strung together and set end to end (figs. 45–49). They are made of very thin nylon mesh, which is partly translucent and thus more or less invisible to fish. Gill nets are not tarred, because unlike trap nets they are lifted every day, but they must be dried frequently. Set at a right angle to the presumed path of fish, the gill net catches fish as they swim through it and are caught by their gills (hence the name of the net and the technique) in the mesh. Although there are legal limits to the size of the mesh, there is some leeway so that fishermen can adjust mesh size to the species of fish they seek. Gill nets may be set either on the lake bottom or closer to the surface, depending upon the traveling habits of different fish species in different areas of the lake at different times of year.

The gill net is pulled into the boat by means of a motorized pulley set inside an open port at the bow of the boat (figs. 50–51). Once inside, the nets are piled into boxes and the crew members remove the fish, one by one, from each net (figs. 52–57). Free of fish, the nets are then sent back out via a similar pulley set inside the stern. Unlike trap-net boats, gill-net *tugs* (as they are locally called) are completely enclosed, so that the time-consuming work of removing fish by hand can be done out of the weather (figs. 58–61).

On Lake Erie, seining is not done in open water, but near the shore of the lake or of the shallow Sandusky Bay toward the lake's western end. A seine net (approximately one-half mile long with a quarter-mile line at each end, foam floats along its top line, and lead weights along its bottom) is towed out in a large arc from the shore seining site by a small boat, which pulls a skiff on which the net has been neatly stacked the afternoon before (figs. 62–64). The net contains a large pouch or "bag" at its center point. The ends of the line are attached to a gasoline-powered double winch on shore, which pulls the arc of line and net toward shore over a three- or four-hour period, gradually drawing the captured fish into the bag (figs. 65–67). When only the bag remains in the water, the float line is lifted above water and hung from stakes as the crew members move a half-submerged skiff next to the staked bag and pass fish into the skiff with dip nets (figs. 68–79). Still in the water, the fish are sorted and then loaded onto pickup trucks for transfer to the fish house or placed on *live trucks* (trucks with aerated tanks for shipping live fish) for shipment to stocked fishing ponds further inland.

The end of any fishing day comes at three or four in the afternoon (or later depending on the number of nets fished that day) at the fish house. Although at one time there were a dozen or so wholesalers along the western Lake Erie shore alone, when we began our work there were only three—Kishman Fish Company in Vermilion, which closed in 1984 to make way for a condominium development, Shore-line Fish Company in Sandusky, and Port Clinton Fish Company in Port Clinton. In the late afternoon, boats and pickups arrive at the fish houses, and the fish they bring, already sorted by species, are conveyor-belted into the building, weighed, re-iced and boxed, some-times filleted, and then shipped via truck to fish markets, distributors, restaurants, and (for lower grade, "junk" fish) chemical and pet-food plants throughout Ohio and the larger region (figs. 80–97).

Whenever the pace of work at a fish house is slack (which is most of the time except the late afternoon), there is much lounging about, joking, card playing, discussion of horse racing and betting, griping, and storytelling. The same sorts of ongoing conversations take place on the boats as well, since there is little to do on either the trip out to the nets or on the trip back (fig. 98), and at seining sites, where only one or two people need keep an occasional eye on the seine's progress toward the shore for the first hour or so.

A good deal of the work of fishing is simple manual labor, easily learned: lifting nets from the water, carrying boxes of fish and ice on and off the boat, loading fish onto trucks, cleaning boats and the like, all of which most fishermen can do reasonably well. When fishermen talk about technique, they naturally talk most about those aspects of the fishing process they consider most important. From our observation of fishermen at work and our interviews with them, these aspects include net design, net making and mending, navigating, finding fish and setting nets so as to catch them, and predicting the weather.

To a large extent these are specialists' skills (especially net work), or at least they are skills not equally shared among fishermen. They require intelligence as well as strength, a combination of qualities cited in stories of notable fishermen (see chapter 3) and crucial to fishermen's occupational identity (see chapter 5). Specialists' skills set them apart and entitle them, in cases where they are not boat owners, to higher status and pay than that given to ordinary crew members. They often keep their knowledge somewhat to themselves, because their livelihood depends upon work that carries their recognized personal "signature." Alva Snell, a retired fisherman from Vermilion, spoke of learning to work on nets.

TL: Did you work on the nets yourself, mend and work nets? How did you learn that skill?
AS: Well, it's something just like anything else. It's just practice. You had to be shown how to start, and it's how well you're smart enough to pick it up faster than the next guy, if you're better than he is or not. After I quit my boat and come down here to Kishman's, just walked down the dock. It was in the fall of the year, brought the nets out in November. The weather wasn't too nice, you know, and one of the fellows down there that had fished with me one time, and he was young, and I had taken him on the boat. He said, "What are you doing?" I said, "Oh, I quit." He hollered to Ray Full, the big boss. "Ray," he says, "hire Alva or I'm quitting." He said, "I'm tired of putting up with some of these fellows that call themselves fishermen." He says, "Go on to work." As soon as I got started there, "Come on in the office. We gotta make some new," what they call cribs, that's the part that the fish is finally cooped up in, and he wanted me to make up the order and make the new cribs, you know. They knew I knew the business. I'm not bragging, but just everybody couldn't do it. It's something that maybe you could do a little mending, but when it comes to making new ones or that, it takes a little bit of know-how. You have to have a pattern, you know, blueprints on different kinds of nets.

TL: If you looked at a net, how would you judge it in terms of quality? You could tell whether somebody didn't know what they're doing made it or somebody that knew what they were doing?
AS: Well, where you find the trouble is when they get mending them. If somebody that don't know what they're doing, they make mistakes. Just like anything else. It has to be so many meshes this way, so many meshes this way, where the tapers, where the net starts to get bigger, you know, it has a certain cut that they make them. And if somebody don't know what they're doing, they make mistakes and botch it up, well, you find it that way. It's just like anything else. If anybody's sewing, you know, whether one person knows what they're doing or whether they are just practicing.

Alva Snell is typical of fishermen who practice one or more of these specialized skills. He is proud of his ability because it sets him apart from other fishermen. In some ways it is what makes him a life-time fisherman, not just someone doing it until another job comes along.

On the other hand, even general tasks and expected responsibilities can be carried out more or less well and accordingly evaluated and appreciated.

Bob Bodi: And another thing, I used to [work in] the twine house, you know. The twine house, and they would bring it [the net] in out of the field. One truck picking it up [to carry it to the lake] and two trucks bringing it in [from storage in the field], and I'd unload it, I and another fellow. And the fellows run the truck together, and I'd get a kick out of a pile [stacked on a truck].
Mrs. Bodi: Straight up and down, just like a house.
BB: Fellows come in from down on the lake, and one of them, and they'd ask Martin, "What did you have, a rim around there?"

Another retired fisherman, Lewis Keller of Marblehead, mentioned how important it was simply to take care of nets—gill nets, in this case—because rotten ones caused fish to be lost.

And jeez, that twine was so damn rotten, you could see all the saugers dropping right back down in the lake. Went along like that for about two weeks. And Jesus Christ, that one week I made twenty-nine dollars. Next week I don't even think I made that much. . . . So, God damn it, this one day he brought down ten boxes of brand new nets. We put them out, the new nets in the boat, we put them out, and we set them. You gotta lift them [gill nets] every day. You can't leave them set like you do a trap net. You put them in, and then you pull them out because the fish are in them. We set these ten boxes of new nets, and I'm telling you, man, I never seen so many saugers in my life. Jesus, them nets was just full of them. Man, they just come up and look like a blanket coming up with saugers. Half the day I'd pick up the nets, and the other half of the day picking the fish out. That week I made some money. [But he] pulled them right out that day, put them on the reel, and didn't put them back in the water no more. They put the old ones back in again, see? I thought the hell with this crap. I had all the fishing I wanted then. I got one good paycheck, and that was it.

Bodi emphasizes his aesthetic pride in doing good work, but Keller stresses the economic advantages; both concerns are important because each leads to the other.

The nets used for all three fishing techniques need to be custom-made by individual fishermen with the necessary skill (often called "twine men" after the fishermen's term for the net material). Their design depends upon a number of biological and geographical factors. While some fishermen may scheme out their trap, gill, or seine net patterns on graph paper, the actual construction of nets—particularly of a 1500-pound, 100-foot-long trap-net structure containing a series of complicated tapers of different angles made by counting "so many meshes over, so many meshes down"—is done largely by memory and by hand in the net yard or shed (fig. 99). In addition, lake turbulence, damage caused in lifting and pulling, and the rotting effects of water make all three sorts of nets, especially the lightweight material used in gill-net fishing, in need of regular repair. During the winter months, on any off day during the season, or even when part of a crew is fishing, someone will be at the crew's net yard or shed, retying broken knots in the mesh, tarring nets, or cutting out and replacing rotted sections of net (figs. 100–106).

Like other specialized fishing skills, net work cannot be learned on one's own. Net design and construction—particularly of the complex trap nets used extensively in western Lake Erie—demand a vast knowledge of the interdependent variables of water, weather, lake geography, fish behavior, fishing technique, and the capabilities of net material (Byington 1984, 23). The design and making of a net requires that knowledge of these variables be incorporated into an actual object, crafted from raw material by hand. Net mending, although less complicated, still requires close attention and special manual dexterity to be done correctly and efficiently. As a result, learning these skills takes more than time. It takes a tradition, which can distill the experience of many individuals into an accepted and manageable set of considerations, and it takes a teacher who can draw on that tradition along with his own personal concern and attention.

We asked Lewis Keller if all fishermen knew how to make trap nets.

LK: No, not all of them. There was only, pert near all the old-timers were pretty handy at that stuff, but you take the younger fellows [of the time] like me, and oh, quite a few young fellows at that time, but they used me for the heavy work and that.

PM: So you didn't learn how to mend nets?

LK: Oh, yes, you learn how to mend, too. Yes, you had to take and learn how to mend the same as the other guys. Only to make up a new net, there was a lot of figuring to do because there was a lot of tapering and all that, and you got to know how to cut that twine to make a taper and fit it together and that, cause that was quite a job.

PM: You didn't just go down and buy a new net. You had to make it yourself there for the fish company.

LK: Oh, yes, you could get the twine, you could get it any depth you wanted. You could get from ten feet up to thirty, thirty-five feet deep. But then, you had different size meshes. Now like for, at that time, you had to have a five-inch mesh for a leader on a net. Then it run from five inches to four inches to three inches, then to two. Then where your tires used to be, you had to know how to sew them because your different sizes would have to, there was a lot of learning to do on that stuff. I was pretty good at it.

PM: How did you learn?

LK: Through my dad. Hell, my dad, he used to make any kind of a net. My dad, he was awful good at making up twine and that, and trimble nets and stuff like that, poop nets.

Chester Jackson, a retired fisherman from Vermilion, had similar attitudes about net making and mending.

CJ: Well, just anybody can't make a trap net. I mean it's very complicated. It would take at least five years to be what you would call a twine man. Take a hunk of webbing from a net company, and assemble one of these trap nets, cause you got your tapers and everything. There's so much. You don't learn it overnight, and you don't learn in a book. You learn from experience and a good teacher. See, I'm left-handed. When I first started down here, everybody's right-handed. I couldn't mend left-handed, you know, where they made the knots. So this old fisherman from, a fellow by the name of Thomas, from Port Clinton, he was working down here. He says, "I'll show you how to mend." Here's another thing: they didn't want to show you. See, they were afraid you would take their job because they may be laid off in the wintertime. You got better than they was, and they would be out of a job, and because you're young, and maybe they were old-fashioned after X number of years, and most of them wouldn't want to teach you cause they guarded their job. And in those days, you didn't have all the benefits you have today. Never did have as far as that goes in the industry. But this fellow, his name was Art (Thomas), he says, "I'll show you." He takes a needle in his left hand. He was an experienced twine man, and hell, he used his left hand. Well, after he showed me how to do it with my left hand, I could do it after a couple lessons, see. That's how I started. If you wasn't able to mend twine, you got laid off in the wintertime. No use for you.

Using these acquired skills also takes intelligence, in particular a combination of observation, forethought, and ingenuity. Changing circumstances on the lake often require changes in the way net work and other fishing activities are done. Successful fishermen need to see these changes coming and to devise new techniques to cope with them. In such cases, once-successful traditional ways of doing things may no longer be useful, and the conservative force of tradition itself, useful though it may be in teaching, can become a hindrance.

The cycle of change is completed when an ingenious innovation, such as the trap net design developed some forty years ago by Martin Hosko and his first twine man, George Bruney, becomes part of the tradition over time. In this occupation as in others, tradition is not static, although it is often spoken of in terms that make it seem so. It may be seen as a way of expressing the current state of workable and accepted knowledge in the occupation. Hosko takes pride of a sort fishermen understand in his attention to detail, which helped him to see the need for a new net design.

MH: When you work in the lake yourself like he [his brother] did, and I did the same thing, you educate yourself. Everytime I built some nets, I lifted them myself. And I had other men lift them during the year, and I watched how well they fished. And the biggest secret was give your mesh smaller cord and make the net lighter, and the [bigger] fish would go in. The little fish had a chance to work out of the net. . . . They was always trying to keep that as small as they could to catch the smaller fish, and then they'd open it up inside the square so the little fish could get out. That's where a lot of them were making their big mistake, but they didn't know it. He wanted to catch that eleven-inch blue pike and eleven-inch sauger, and the net was too dark for pickerel to go in or pike fish, even blue pike. Now the bigger mesh and smaller cord, the other [smaller] fish would get out, and it wasn't loaded with a bunch of, I call them trash, where you got a bunch of undersize fish [which take extra time to throw back] and it gets crowded. The good fish couldn't work into the net [if it was full of smaller fish]. It was so simple, but it was awful hard for a fish company to see what the man was doing wrong. The fishermen wanted the small mesh because he didn't have to reach out and pick out any gilled fish, see?

Larry Davis, an active trap netter from Vickery, west of Sandusky, gives Hosko and Bruney what is now their accepted place in local fishing tradition. His high opinion of their nets is based on practical, traditional, and aesthetic definitions of "good work."

This area right here has basically got the same type of [trap] net. . . . I'm talking about a design that I guess George Bruney and Martin Hosko developed this particular net that we're all using yet. Oh, back in the mid 40s, and we're still at the same design. They tried to change them, and they haven't come up with anything nearly as good as what we've been fishing with, so I've never tried to change. I guess I'm from the old school. If I've got something that's working, I'm not gonna mess with it.

LD: George was his, Martin's twine man. And then when George left Hosko, he built nets for everybody else. He's been gone now, I think George died about 1973 or 1974. But he built I think pert near every net that I own, and he was an excellent twine man. He was a perfectionist. If in a hundred feet, he was off a quarter of an inch, he cut it off, and started all over again. That's the kind of worker he was.

TL: That's the kind of a net you want.

LD: Yes, but that guy, he was a perfectionist, and very good.

Although good work is necessary for good catches, it is good not only for practical reasons, but also because it can be appreciated for its own sake and for the aesthetic pleasure given by work done better than it needs to be done. While fishermen certainly appreciate the praise of other fishermen—coming as it does from those who should know—perhaps a greater pleasure comes from within, as evidenced by Hosko and his friend and second twine man, Bob Bodi.

BB: So Martin come in and he said, "Bob, you go mending the twine, go mending the twine. George left us." So from then on, I adjusted all the bailing cribs and other work there. Whatever there was to do. And Martin a lot of times would be in the office, and I'd go and get him or motion to him, and he'd come in there and approve it. You'd just get a kick of something like that. See how your net would stretch up in there just like it would be in the lake, we did [see figs. 17–20].

BB: On a nice day, I think the most enjoyment I ever got out of life was to see that string of twine [a net] setting there perfect like that, and you could take a tape measure, anybody could go out there. And I bet there wasn't anything six inches out of the way. . . .
MH: Big nets would reach about a mile. But we'd have a range and we'd run the anchors off. When we got through setting up the nets, I'd run full length of the string [run the boat back along the nets just set]. I'd see the net setting up nice, and it done the same thing to me, Bob. It sort of thrilled me more than you because it was mine, but it just give me a lift when I get through running and see how nice a job we did setting them up. That string of net, that one mile, wouldn't be out a foot. It didn't have to be that nice.

As William Wilson has pointed out, work done this well is not simply decorative as well as utilitarian; it responds to the deeper human need to make "aesthetically satisfying patterns" that is at the root of all art (1988, 158–59). Bodi's and Hosko's statements evidence this same point: creating such work goes beyond achievement in technique. It puts technique in the service of personal emotion and occupational pride.

As with netmaking, not all fishermen master navigational skills. These are usually the province of the boat owner or of an experienced crew member. Once again, many variables must be taken into account through both traditional practice and individual systems of observation. Even with buoys and sometimes with navigational equipment, considerable ability can be required to run a boat to any trap or gill net site when the shore is too distant to act as a guide and when sky and water visually blend together, as they often do. Fishermen use landmarks on shore, buoys at the end of their nets, timing and compasses to find nets that are ready to be lifted, but frequent fog and bad weather can make the process more difficult, and allowances must always be made for mechanical variation and human error.

Chester Jackson: Everybody had different markers. My wife remarks today how what good eyesight I have for distant reading, like road signs and stuff. When you work on the water, I guess your eyes develop a certain, I don't know, long distance focus is what it is. You know, you had some of your crew, some of the crew couldn't see a buoy if it was across the street. I could see them sometimes for maybe a half a mile. See, everything is timing and course. Everything is set time and course. I mean, when you get outside the sight of land, that's a big body of water out there. It doesn't look like it, but it really is. If you don't have your compass course, and of course, so much on our boat that would throw the compass off, where you placed your gear. Now these compasses on these big freighters, that are almost a hundred percent accurate, but the fish boats aren't. You gotta make a lot of allowances. You got the current in the water. That will side slip your boat. You got to take all this into consideration. You missed your nets, but then you run your time, and of course, you always know where the other fellows were setting, and you try to keep that all in your memory, so eventually you find them.

PM: You mean sometimes you go out there and you can't find them?

CJ: Yes, if it's foggy or a little bit hazy, you don't see too far, and you gotta be—these compasses on these fish boats aren't as accurate as your big freighters, you know. I know one day there's a joke down here, this was years ago. He worked for me one time, fellow by the name of Mellman [not his real name]. He was gone all day and come back in and didn't have a fish aboard. He run around there all day and never found his nets. I would have felt like a fool if I would have come aboard and come back that afternoon with no fish.

Lewis Keller: You can get lost coming back awful easy. Just like, when I run boats for Brown's down here, I used to run one twenty-six footer, and on foggy days when it was so foggy you couldn't get the mail plane over to the island, well they used to bring the mail down, and I used to run the mail over to the island. And I would take and set that compass on my course, hit the dock everytime, run my time out, and load it up, and the damn dock will loom right up in front of you. And then coming back, reverse it, and I could come right back to where I started, see? But then, the boat broke down one day, so I had to take another one. And it had a different type compass on. It had, well, one is filled with fluid, and one is a dry compass. Well, this was a dry compass. Well, going over to Kelleys Island, hit it right on the nose. Coming back, I run my time out, and God damn, something's wrong here. So, I run in just a little closer, still no land. Then I went about five minutes one way, didn't see nothing, come back, then went five minutes the other way. Couldn't see nothing, come back, then I went back in, started going in again. So the third time I went in, Jesus, all of a sudden, these trees like this loomed right up in front of me. I set in pert near right on the beach. That's how thick it was that morning. And then I knew right away where I was. I knew them trees. Here, instead of coming up, instead of coming into Lakeside, I was clear up in East Harbor. That's how much that compass was out coming back.

Here again we see how mastery of a specialized work skill is the source of occupational identity and a cause for pride. Even though Lewis Keller becomes lost in his story, he is lost because of his reliance on an inaccurate compass, and he knows just where he is when he reaches land. His story attests to his navigational skill, which he sees as an element in what makes him a fisherman. Chester Jackson's story contrasts his ability to navigate with that of Mellman, who cannot even achieve the primary goal of every fisherman: to bring back fish from the lake. If Mellman cannot do this, he must not be a real fisherman.

Successful fishermen also need to know where to set their nets: where fish of many species are most likely to be in different areas and depths of the lake under various weather conditions and throughout the season. In order to do so, they refer to a great store of information remembered from past seasonal cycles, modified by their own and others' observation in the days and weeks just before. Martin Hosko kept detailed written records of locations and catches for decades.

MH: Well, you know by year after year where you done your best fishing and what time. I sort of kept track of when. I think I sounded pert near every foot of the lake certain depth through Detroit River clear to [names an Ohio town]. Now the nicest ground in the summertime was outside of Vermilion about northeast. There was a black sand out there. It was deep water, and it was a sandbar about seven miles and then it started deepening off about sixty feet. Right outside of that, right when it sloped, and the slope was for about two miles long, the sand was black, black as coal.

Chester Jackson's recollections show the importance of recognizing seasonal cycles on the lake and changes in those cycles over time.

Well, different species would be more predominant than others. But, if we had a bad spring, we would have a good fall. There was something always to be caught. Of course, blue pike, if you wanted blue pike, you went to Conneaut, Ashtabula, Fairport to catch your blue pike. Below Cleveland. And they seemed to like the deeper water, see, it's deeper water down there. [Though Cleveland and these other towns are actually "up" from (north and east of) the western lake, western fishermen speak of them as being "down."] I don't know, but in the summer we would catch them out here. We always planned our nets so around the first of May, 15th of May, we'd set outside the blue pike. You'd get blue pike and whitefish, just pure blue pike and whitefish. And, of course, then the perch would come on. Now, perch wasn't always predominantly heavy either. When I started in the 30s they had a run of perch here. That's before I got started. In '31, '32, and '33 there was a heavy run of perch. Then they tapered off. Then it seems like the pickerel, blue pike, and that stuff came along. But there was always edible fish to be caught which now we don't have.

Despite this store of information, there is still an element of chance in the endeavor, which was also fueled by competition among crews and boats.

PM: How would you know where to find fish? Where to look?
Chester Jackson: Well, you know, that's something that you learn from experience. You don't always get the right answers— just going back when I'd say Alva [Snell] and I were rivals. He had his company, and at the time I was working for Parson's. That's the same company here. We set nets out there. We were lifting, this was the day we was lifting, and he come up and he says, "How's fishing?" I says, "There's nothing here." He went five

minutes northwest of me, set his nets, and three or four days later when we went out to lift again, we still didn't have nothing, and he had about a ton of nice pickerel in the nets he just set. I mean it's a hit and a miss. And, of course, it's worked the other way, too. I've set in the fish where somebody else wasn't getting them. Just, that's the challenge of it. That's the challenge of it.

PM: So you use your experience to determine where they are, but still it's a chance? You're not sure there are going to be any fish.

CJ: Of course, we never had depth finders or fish finders like they have today. They've got all the mechanical. Never had that stuff. You knew certain places was good at certain times of the year. Something you learned. You just didn't learn it from a book.

The element of chance makes finding fish more of a challenge to the fisherman, but he responds with ingenuity based on his knowledge accumulated through years of experience. In many ways, a fisherman's occupational identity becomes more deeply ingrained the longer he has been fishing.

Weather is an extremely important factor in commercial fishing, which affects both the economic success of fishing trips and the safety of fishermen and boats on the lake. Although lake fishing trips rarely last more than a day, and boats stay relatively close to shore, Lake Erie is a shallow lake, and it can become turbulent quickly and seemingly without notice. Like fishermen elsewhere, those on Lake Erie rely on a combination of official weather reports and informal folk knowledge to give themselves advance notice of bad weather.

Chester Jackson: Weather is the most important part of it. You plan your work ahead. To be successful, you have to plan ahead several days, whether you're going to lift, pull, set, mend, tar your gear. There's always work to do, but since they got the weather on t.v., and it's much better today. Today I can watch that weather on t.v. and predict whether it will be here three days, not one hundred percent accurate, but pretty accurate. By watching the high and low pressure systems, the data they give you on t.v. today is fantastic.

Luke Gowitzka: Sometimes if you fish at the lake, go out in the evening, all the lights in the whole lake, all the lights from the island, the lights would really be kind of real bright, you know. You just knew she was gonna blow from the north, so you just hoped to stay out of it and not get caught. Once in awhile, we'd go anyhow. That's how we find out.

PM: Were there other signs like that to help you tell what the weather was gonna be like?

LG: Maybe the water where you was walking, maybe the water in about ten minutes would swell, and you knew that there was something working out in the lake. That would scare you.

Lewis Keller: Well, you could tell which way the wind was blowing, like southwest, south, or southeast winds. Any wind that comes out of the south or west, you could lift Cedar Point or someplace, but out of the northeast, there was no place you could lift because you couldn't get out there to lift because that was coming clear across the lake. But on your other winds, though, you used to go out in pretty nasty weather though to lift nets, regardless, even in northeasters. Used to have to get the fish out, or the fish would drown.

As in other areas of fishing practice, pragmatism seems to be the ruling principle in the fishermen's system of weather prediction: if it works, use it. They watch weather forecasts on television but combine this with traditional weather signs in order to plan their fishing activities. This traditional knowledge is more important than weather forecasts in shaping occupational identity. Anyone can get a forecast from television or radio, but only commercial fishermen know about bright lights, water swells, and wind direction as weather indicators.

Two young, still active commercial fishermen, Joe Herr, thirty-eight, and Paul Leidorf, forty-five, seem to depend on weather signs more than some of the retired fishermen did.

JH: There's a lot of people ask you what you're going to do. Yes, but the weatherman says it's going to be nice. Stick around for a little bit, and we'll see.

PM: You can tell just by looking?

JH: Seldom ever wrong.

PL: You can look up and see the clouds.

PM: You have to get a feeling for it?

PL: You pay more attention to that than you do the national weather.

JH: The fish will tell you, too, if there's weather coming. They know three days ahead of time what's coming. You got a bad roll coming and you handle the fish, and they're excited. Flippy flopping all over the place, and they're spooky. They want to get out of there. Uh, oh, we got something coming. Day and a half or two days.

PL: Forty-eight hour period.

JH: Before the weatherman knows about it, the fish know about it.

Since Herr and Leidorf are out on the lake every day, they need as much knowledge of the weather as they can get, including official weather forecasts and weather signs. They recognize that the weather forecasts can be wrong, and they have a stronger belief in the efficacy of signs. This belief is based on both observed results and on the importance of belief to identity. Because they see themselves as working close to nature, their belief in natural signs reinforces this part of their own identity.

Although experience, watchfulness, and weather reports or signs help to keep fishermen safe from the hazards of work on the lake, supernatural help can also be called upon. Martin Hosko and several other retired fishermen, for instance, mentioned the traditional prohibition against fishing on Fridays (Mullen 1978b, 6), although none of them totally believed in the practice. A few trap-net boats carry St. Christopher medals above their wheels (Mullen 1978b, 22), and some Catholic crew members wear them. Joe Herr mentioned another good luck practice.

JH: See these up here? You'll see a penny behind every one of these window braces. Every crew member comes out of the bay, he puts a penny up here. That way he's always got something to bring back. Always.

PM: Every crew member? You tell them to put their penny up there?

JH: When they quit, they take their penny with them.

PM: Where'd you get that?

JH: Two old-timers. Real old-timers. Find a spot to stick a penny. A nice spot.

PM: What's it mean? It means that if they—

JH: That means that she's always going to bring you back. The boat owes you that penny. The boat owes you, see? You don't owe the boat nothing; it owes you cause it's got your penny. See, it's gonna bring you back. She always does, so far.

This kind of folk belief is common among deep sea fishermen the world over (Bassett 1885; Malinowski 1948; Mullen 1978b; Poggie and Gersuny 1972), but only a handful of Lake Erie commercial fishermen reported such superstitions. The lack of a more extensive magic folk belief system among Lake Erie fishermen can be explained by the relative safety of their work when compared to fishermen who venture out into the North Atlantic or the Gulf of Mexico. Lake Erie fishermen are out in the lake for only a day at a time, they are usually within sight of land, and other boats are often nearby. This contrasts to the week- to month-long trips made by deep sea fishermen when they are out of sight of land and other boats. The risks involved in ocean fishing cause fishermen to have anxiety that can be relieved by belief in magic that gives them some sense of psychological control over the uncertain situation. This explanation is based on the anxiety-ritual theory (Malinowski 1948), and it helps to explain why Lake Erie fishermen have relatively few superstitions: they do not face the same risks and uncertainties that ocean fishermen do. The superstitions they do have are isolated among individuals and are not part of their shared occupational lore.

Most of the customs of commercial fishermen indicate shared knowledge and group identity, but at least one area of custom has the potential for conflict. Although seiners own or rent the shore sites from which they fish, trap and gill netters do not have particular rights to specific fishing areas. Although a certain courtesy governs the setting of nets, independence and competition for a livelihood make this a less than perfect, although workable, system.

> **TL:** The size of the area that you think about when you're setting up trap nets is pretty large. If you've got a lot of them, that's a pretty wide area. How is it decided whose area is whose?
> **Larry Davis:** Trial and error. I mean, fellows learn the areas they want to fish in. You have people try and crowd you out with a handful of fishermen. We have this year in and year out. We have a couple individuals who are kinda nasty about the way they want to set nets, but—
> **TL:** Ideally, everybody would recognize everybody else's area.
> **LD:** That would be ideal, but it probably will never happen. Cause that's the nature of the fishermen. They're all ornery individuals as a rule.

Many fishermen *are* ornery individuals, or individualists at the very least (being "your own boss" is one of the attractions of the work), and this makes for some conflict within the occupational group. In general, though, fishermen still have a sense of themselves as a group set apart—sometimes by their "orneryness" but more often by their skills—from others in the community. Despite any differences they might have about fishing rights in certain areas, their similarities in terms of shared knowledge are far more important in shaping their occupational identity.

One traditional custom has been so much a part of a fishermen's everyday life for so long that they have come to take it for granted. Fishermen's wives are more likely to recall this custom because it, unlike many other aspects of the occupation, involves their work. Because the fishing boats are out on the lake for an entire day, most fishermen take their lunches with them. Several wives of fishermen mentioned that their husbands used special lunch buckets, larger than the lunch box usually associated with factory workers (fig. 14). Chester Jackson's wife remembered the huge lunches he used to take out.

Another thing about him and his lunches. He never had lunch, it was always roasted meat, home made bread, home made pies. Everything was home made from scratch. Everything.
PM: For him to take out on the boat for his lunch?
Mrs. J: I've still got his old lunch bucket. It's about that big around, you know, one of those great big old. It's metal and stands about that high. He had that son-of-a-gun loaded with sandwiches.
PM: The kind with the thermos in the top?
Mrs. J: Well, they had a little tray in the top.
Mr. J: Miner's bucket. Coal miner's bucket.
Mrs. J: But he had that son-of-a-gun loaded. And then he would come home and eat a whopper of a meal, too, on top of that.
Mr. J: I'm a big eater yet.

The traditional role of a fisherman's wife called for her to provide food for her husband and sometimes for other men who worked with him. The wives we interviewed often mentioned the tremendous amounts of food their husbands ate and the work it was for wives to cook it. Bob Bodi's wife fed an entire crew.

No matter what you put on the table, they just licked it right up. Well, they were hungry, you know. They had been out in the lake, and it wasn't that part of the season. Well, they would have to repair their nets and tar them. Can you imagine taking a big old net . . . and have it with tar and then you gunk all that netting in that tar. Now, it was hard work, but they liked it.

Emma Gowitzka prepared food for thirteen men who worked for the seining operation of her husband Luke.

EG: We used to fish around the clock. I used to cook for as high as thirteen men when they fished. We had to haul all the food and all the water up to Crystal Point.
LG: We could fish day and night then.
EG: Five in the morning I'd cook breakfast for them, and then they'd start out fishing.
PM: And you would take all those meals out there?
EG: I took it right there. I took the food along and cooked it.
PM: And then dinner in the middle of the day?
EG: Yes.
LG: She helped fish for a year or two.
EG: I helped fish, and I cooked. I don't think there's ever been a seine sew that I didn't help on till this last one. Used to sew all the seines.
PM: What kind of food did you make when you went out there?
EG: Regular dinner. Potatoes.
PM: Potatoes and pork chops, and?
EG: Yes, potatoes, pork chops, and a vegetable, and then a lot of times I caught fish, I fried fish. They like the fish for sure. They would hurry up and clean them for me so I'd fry them.

The testimony of Mrs. Jackson, Mrs. Bodi, and Mrs. Gowitzka indicates that even an everyday custom has meaning for occupational identity. Fishermen see themselves as hard-working outdoorsmen, and their prodigious eating habits fit right in with this self-image. They worked hard all day, and they naturally had big appetites. This also links them to American working-class heroes who are known as big eaters (Mullen 1978b, 124). Whether they helped out with other fishing tasks, fishermen's wives share in this particular feature of occupational identity, because they prepared the meals and seem proud of their husbands' appetites as well as of their own cooking abilities.

Fishermen's wives also had to share in certain unpleasant aspects of the fishing occupation, some of which are based on stereotypes about the life of fishing families. All the guests of a fisherman's wife expected fish dinners from her, as Mrs. Jackson recalled.

But everybody that came to our house, I had to fry fish for them. I got so sick of frying fish. Skillets, you know, about five pounds, and I did it all in skillets. We didn't have deep fryers then. But everybody wanted fish and potato salads.

If a fisherman's life was hard, so was his wife's; she had to deal with fish too, if more indirectly.

PM: What about your point of view as the wife of a fisherman?
Mrs. Jackson: I still can't stand the smell of fish. You know, he always smelled so terrible, you know, it would be soaked in his sleeves. Some of it, you know, was from rotten fish.
Mr. J: Oh, you would come home stinking.
Mrs. J: It was hard to get it out of his clothing.

Overall, the wives contributed greatly to their husbands' work and helped to create and reinforce their positive occupational identity.

Commercial fishermen's occupational techniques and customs are learned traditionally from the first time out in the lake and continue to be refined throughout working life. The process of occupational teaching and learning maintains both the work traditions and the identity of fishermen. What they know as fishermen sets them apart from other people at the same time that it joins them together as a group. Without this shared knowledge of technique and custom, there would be no occupational identity; in fact, there would be no occupation. As fishermen's comments reveal, this body of knowledge involves more than practical knowledge; it also includes occupational judgement, aesthetics, and pride in skills that require special abilities. Fishermen who can make and mend nets, navigate a boat in bad weather, find where the fish are located, and predict the weather accurately are the best fishermen, the ones who maintain the core occupational identity, who define what it means to be a fisherman.

2

The Past

Lewis Keller, a seventy-five year old retired trap-net fisherman, likes
to sit at Turinsky's dock at Marblehead and talk with younger men
about his experiences on Lake Erie. The listeners have work to do
and have heard many of the stories before so that his opportunities
to reminisce with a group are limited. He is no longer in contact
with the men he used to fish with: some have died, and the others
live across Sandusky Bay in Sandusky, not far away but far enough
to be inconvenient to visit. Thus, he was pleased to sit on the front
porch of his old stone house (built in 1796 and known locally as
"the old stone fort") on Marblehead Peninsula and be interviewed
by a folklorist interested in the old days of commercial fishing on
Lake Erie. Many of the retired fishermen we interviewed were like
Lewis Keller in that they enjoyed talking about the old days but did
not have many opportunities to do so.

Another retired fisherman, seventy-five-year-old Alva Snell, has had
more chances than Keller to talk about the old days because he operates
a fish cleaning business in Vermilion and comes in contact with the
public all day during the sport fishing season. He also occasionally sees
other retired fishermen who live nearby. For instance, Snell regularly
sees and reminisces with Chester Jackson, one of his friends and co-
workers from his fishing days.

PM: Do you get much of a chance to talk to him [Jackson]?
AS: Oh yes.
PM: When you get together and talk, do you talk about your
days as commercial fishermen?
AS: Of course, not so much now. We've talked it all over a

number of times, but we will, when something will come up, we
will say, you know, well, so and so if they would have done it a
little different, they would have made out a little better or something. They were half trying or they don't know what they're
doing. That outfit down at Kishman's now, we talk about it all the
time. Hell, if we were there, we'd be catching some fish. They got
a job, and that's all they care about.

PM: Did you ever tell some of these experiences like, well, recall
the time that such and such happened?

AS: Oh, yes. It comes up, you know. If that's been your life,
well, things come up that's happened during your lifetime that
either was funny or sad.

Jackson, who is sixty-nine, described the situation in a similar way.
"The only one I see is Alva. Very few men left around here. See, Alva
Snell and myself is about the only two trap-netters left."

Retired fishermen live in different towns along the Western Basin.
Many of them knew each other during their days of active fishing, but
they are no longer in contact. For instance, Snell and Jackson knew
Martin Hosko of Toledo, but they have not seen him since they
retired. Hosko occasionally visits with Bob Bodi, who worked for him
for twenty-one years. We interviewed the two of them together in
Bodi's front yard in Toledo. They were both trap-netters, and usually
the men in one kind of fishing were more familiar with other men in
that line: trap-netters associated with trap-netters and did not know
many gill-netters. Luke Gowitzka is a retired seiner, and he did not
know any trap- or gill-netters.

These six men—Keller, Snell, Jackson, Hosko, Bodi, and Gowitzka—were all retired, and they all enjoyed talking about their occupational past. Their identities as fishermen continued to be strong after
they were no longer actively fishing or spending much time with other
fishermen. Why does occupational identity continue to exert such a
powerful influence on these individuals? Their occupational personal
experience narratives reveal certain patterns and attitudes that help
to explain the maintenance of job-related identities. There were three
recurring themes in the stories of retired fishermen about the past
(some of these form separate narrative categories but they all overlap):
starting-out experiences, family tradition, and the most pervasive
topic, a contrast between the past and the present. When talking about
the old days, retired fishermen always presented the past as better, as

a "golden age" (Santino 1978). There were five subthemes in the "golden age" stories: more primitive technology, harder work, clearer water, more abundant fish, and less governmental restriction. Certainly some aspects of fishing were better in the past, but we must recognize that these elderly fishermen are romanticizing the past to a certain extent much as retirees from other occupations do, or for that matter, as human beings in general do.

Every retired fisherman we interviewed remembered the circumstances in which he first began commercial fishing. With several men this was related to a family occupational tradition, as in Lewis Keller's case.

PM: Well, how long have you been involved in fishing?
LK: Since I was fourteen years old, and I'm going on seventy-six right now. So, I've been around it a little bit. I started out fishing with my dad, and my dad was a commercial fisherman. That was years ago, and at that time years ago there were five fish companies in Sandusky. There was the Lay Brothers, United Fisheries, the Worley Fishery, Schock Fishery, and the Food Fishery. Five big fisheries in town there at one time, and I worked for, well, when I went to work for my dad, it was during the First World War, and men were hard to get. They were scarce; you couldn't hire men because fishing, there was, well, you could say, it didn't pay too much. It was cheap labor in a way, but even men were hard to get at that time, but even if guys had a job, they still had a job anyway at that. I was pretty good size already, and I begged him to take me fishing, so I went and he took me along. We went out, and pulled nets, and those days you didn't have reels and motors that done the work for you. You done it all by hand. You had to reach over there and pull that net aboard, then force it aboard, and that was a lot of work at that time. And I fished with them, well, until they found a man. I ended up going with them for maybe a month, and I was pretty young for that kind of work at that time, and I went back fishing, I can't remember just how old I was.

Despite the fact that he was just a boy at the time, he remembers many of the details, such as the names of the fishing companies in Sandusky. The beginning point of one's life's work is so significant that even toward the end of life, a person can vividly remember the circumstances. The other important factor in Keller's narration is that his father was the one who first took him out on a boat. His occupational identity is even more firmly entrenched because it is related to family identity: there is a blood tie to his work.

Like Keller, Alva Snell spoke of how family tradition prompted him to start fishing.

> Well, this is a fishery that was in Grand River they call it. And my father was a commercial fisherman, my grandfather was a commercial fisherman, my great-grandfather was a commercial fisherman, so it's just natural that I do it, of course. My father was running a boat, and I went with him on a boat. Those days there was lots of herring in the lake. That was the first job a boy would get going out in the lake. They would cut the herring down the middle, scrape the insides out. That way when you got to shore, they were all ready to be shipped for smoked fish. That's what they did with them, and that way you didn't have to do it ashore, which would delay the process, you know. And, so I worked that year and every other summer till I got through high school, and as soon as I got through high school—you know how it is—a boy wants to leave home, and they called from here, Kishman's, a fishery in Grand River, and wanted to know if there was any boys down there that wanted to go out in the lake and clean fish, and of course, that was me. "Yes, I'll take it." So I came and went to work on one of the boats. Well, then the next year, the captain of the boat called me and wanted me to work on the boat. So, I've been here ever since. Not cleaning fish, but he wanted me as a crew member, you know. And so there's been a lot of changes.

Again we see the vivid memory for details—the exact technique for cleaning herring—and the emphasis on family tradition. Snell frames the story with a litany of his ancestors who were involved in commercial fishing, thus placing himself in this family continuum. His history is also similar to Keller's in that both started work at a very young age.

At an even earlier age, Snell worked in the fishing industry "putting up" ice.

> Well, anyway, I was a young boy in World War I, and I remember the principal of the school and the people that ran the fisheries coming up to the school and asked all the seventh and eighth grade boys to stand up. When they all stood up, they said you, you, you to such and such a fish house, and you, you, you. They had to put up ice because so many young men had gone to war, and they had to get the ice up. In those days they took it out of

the lake or river, and they had to get it. Otherwise, there would be no fish the next year. They didn't have ice machines like they have today, so they didn't have enough help, so they got seventh and eighth grade boys, and even women were putting up ice. I worked in a fish house when I was thirteen years old after school and in the summertime, and started out in the lake when I was fourteen years old. That's 1918. The boys hadn't all got home, you know. And anybody who would go out in the lake, they would take them. Took me out in the lake in 1918.

In both Snell's and Keller's starting-out stories, there are comparisons between yesterday and today: Snell mentions that they did not have ice machines back then, and Keller says that they had to pull in the nets by hand, not with machines. They both repeat phrases such as "those days" and "at that time" to emphasize the distance between the present storytelling and the events being described in the story. These themes of contrast are found throughout all of the other narrative categories of retired fishermen.

Because Alva Snell's father, grandfather, and great-grandfather were all commercial fishermen, he has a strong personal sense of the tradition. Interestingly, he learned many of the family fishing experiences from his grandmother.

TL: Do you have any idea about when it was that your grandfather started fishing?
AS: Oh, close to it. I've got a picture of it here when he was born. I can tell you. Let's see. I can't find it right now, but I think he was born in 1840. I know my grandmother was quite a bit younger than he was, and she said she was a big enough girl during the Civil War so she remembered some of the Civil War. When she married my grandfather, he was running a schooner here on the lake. She went on the boat as cook. And then he got the job running the fishery up there in Fairport Harbor. So he died when I was real young. Just how many years he fished I couldn't tell you. He died when I was about three.

Great-grandfather, that would be my grandmother's father. They lived on the lake bank just this side of Fairport. She says she can remember him—my grandmother was telling me this, the one that lived to be ninety-three—said she can remember him working all winter long making nets ready for spring. They would fish in the spring until the weather got so he could do the farming, and then he would farm, and then fish again in the fall.

This story is important because it links Snell's identity to three previous generations; his occupational identity comes not only from his father, but from his grandmother's father as well. Lewis Keller was the only other fishermen we interviewed who described fishing in the nineteenth century as he had heard about it from his father.

Martin Hosko, seventy-eight, told a story about how he got started in fishing, which also involved family, but his narrative is also an ethnic immigration story.

My father come from Czechoslovakia in 1890, and he come with his brother, and his brother went on to California, and my father went to Columbus. He went back and forth four times, and he made these baskets for summertime and flowers and stuff, wire baskets. I guess he had a pretty good business in Columbus. And every time he stayed about a year or so, a year and a half, and make a little money, he would go back to the old country, in Czechoslovakia, and purchase a little land, and every time he come he'd want a little more. Finally, last time he come here in 1900, he went back and forth four times, in 1900 because I was born in 1905. The last time he come here about 1900, or 1901 or '02. Then he sent for Mother. Then, of course, I come and meantime, my mother she brought my brother who was about eighteen years older than me. And I was three years old when he was talking about going back to the old country, my mother and dad. And I guess they thought they had money enough made to live pretty good over there.

So my brother run away from home. They was going to take him with them, and he come to Cleveland. . . . And when he got off down here at Bayshore Road, that's where most of the fishermen went fishing. That was back in 1907 because he run away from home about a week before they was ready to go. And so that is how he got over here and got fishing. So he started fishing with fishermen, and then he went into business for himself. Must have been in, before 1910 because when I was twelve years old, I went to school for five years. That was as far as you could go in school then. I would end up going quite a ways on the train to go to high school, and we couldn't afford that, so I stayed home.

So, my brother never wrote to Mother. My mother never knew for ten years what happened to him. After he run off, he was afraid they would pick him up. See, he wasn't an American citizen because he was born over there. . . . So, when I was twelve years old, he started writing me letters; he was in business in the Ward's

Canal over here. He was married and had a family and had a nice fishery there. He was quite successful catching fish, so we got writing back and forth. So I come when I was fifteen years old. So I never went to school here. I went to work. So that's how I went to work for my brother for ten years.

This is as much a family immigration story as it is an occupational starting-out story; the characters are all family members, and the details document how the family first settled in America. Occupational stories can contain both individual and group concerns and, in this case, more than one group concern. Hosko has an occupational identity as a fisherman, but he also has an ethnic identity as a Czech. As in the stories of Keller and Snell, though, a family member is responsible for getting a boy involved in the occupation.

Hosko and his friend and co-worker Bob Bodi fished together for twenty-one years, and Bodi had already been working as a fisherman for twenty-seven years before that. At eighty-six, he was the oldest fisherman we interviewed. As we sat with him, his wife, and Hosko in Bodi's front yard in Toledo, he related how he started out fishing in 1914.

BB: I was home mostly with my dad, and he was a hard worker. God bless his old heart. But he didn't know what a day's work was. We was in the barn at five in the morning, and we would leave there around about nine at night, and we got our cows milked, horses taken care of, and everything. And as I said to my dad just a little bit earlier than this. It was in July. I said to him, "Dad, there must be an easier way for us to make a living."
MH: Learned the hard work of fishermen. That was easier.
BB: I knew a fellow by the name of Dan, and I asked him then if he would need anybody in the fall. "Yes," he said, "I need one man." I said, "Will you give me a job?" "Yes, be glad to." So I told my dad, "I will stay with you till the harvest is over, and I'm going fishing." "Okay, Son, but remember that's long, hard work." He didn't care cause I went, but I stuck it out, and then to learn to mend twine. Some can pick it up easy, and others will never make it.

So when we got the twine in the twine house that fall, we had a good fall, lot of whitefish and other fish. Man said, "Do you want to work for me this spring?" I said, "I'd love to" because he gave me thirty dollars a month and my board, and I saved every dollar of it that I possibly could because of that long winter. And he said,

"If you want to work for me this spring," he said, "you ain't got nothing to do right now." He said, "I'll give you fifty cents a day and your board to learn to mend this winter." That made me fifteen dollars a month and my board for the winter. And then I worked for him until World War [One] broke out, and I went into the Navy. And I come back from the Navy, I come back on a Friday. He was looking for men to tar, and he wanted me. Friday night I walked up to what they called a saloon, but it was dry. They had cider and soft drinks and stuff like that. And they said, "Are you home to stay?" I said, "Yes." He said, "Come to work for me in the morning." I said, "No, I won't go to work for you in the morning, but I'll be there Monday morning." "Good enough," he says. Then I worked for him till he retired and went up to Michigan to raise onions. And I never left Crane Creek. I went to work for a fellow by the name of Mr. Byars, and he was an old, a real old fisherman, one of the oldest at that time.

Bob Bodi did not learn to fish from his father or any family member, but his father had an important influence on his life: this story exemplifies the value that his father passed on to him of the importance of hard work to a satisfied life. In the series of events that lead up to his becoming a fisherman permanently, Bodi emphasizes that he was rehired because he was a reliable hard worker. Ironically, he left farming because the work was hard, but as his father accurately warned him, fishing was just as hard.

Luke Gowitzka fished seines all of his life in the industry; his story about getting started is unique in that it involves an omen.

LG: I tried to learn fishing in '39, and we had gotten in the war with Japan. That was 1941. And we went selling our fish alive to all these lakes. I'm the guy that started that in this area. I know. I had a real good business here. In fact, it kept me in business all of that year, I was selling the live ones. Dead fish didn't bring very much. We were selling alive to all these people. We really had a good business, and they kept me alive. Kept me in the business anyhow.

PM: Did you seine or did you do trap netting or gill netting?

LG: Seine.

PM: Where do you do your seining?

LG: Crystal Point here in Sandusky.

PM: That's just out west of the bridges, right?

LG: Yes, in Sandusky Bay. Oh, it was a good living. We had a hard way to go, you know. And I did a good job. I met a couple old fellows that quit fishing over at Crystal Point, and they wanted to trap too. They wanted to sell me the outfit, so I said well, I didn't know about it, but my brother could sell twine. So I come home and my mother said, well, they wanted to sell me this rig. I told my mother, and she said that night she had a dream. She said, "Luther, you go buy that outfit. It's a good thing." She said, "I dreamed last night that you were standing on the peak of a barn with your arms out like you were boss, and all the fields were green around." She said, "You go buy that rig." So I bought it. Her dream come true. I've had a lot of good luck. Of course, right now I'm getting pushed around too much. I can't work any more.

Luke Gowitzka's story again brings a family member into the process of becoming a fishermen; his mother's dream was instrumental in his going into fishing. If a person does not have a father in fishing, then it seems that he needs the blessing of a parent in order to succeed in the business. Bob Bodi had the support of his father, and Luke Gowitzka had the urging of his mother. The symbolism of her dream is significant: the farm imagery of barn and green fields is a reminder of a metaphor fishermen often use: that they are harvesting the sea. The element of luck enters into Gowitzka's narrative more than in the others, but this is appropriate because an omen was the beginning point for him. Most fishermen stress hard work as the essential element to success, but they all recognize that luck plays a part.

As mentioned above, every retired fisherman we interviewed contrasted the past with the present. They all spoke of how hard the work was in the old days as compared to today. Lewis Keller mentioned how much of the work was done by hand.

They didn't have the machinery that done the work or nothing like that. Everything was by hand. You worked ten hours a day, six days a week, twenty-nine bucks for a week's wages! That's rough, you know. It's a tough game. I don't give a damn what you say about fishing. Anybody that thinks fishing is easy, even with the equipment they've got today, there's a lot of work to it. But now, they've got these reels for their boats. Hell, they can get everything comes over the top and reel into the boat. Years ago, you used to have to haul with all hand power. It used to be work, boy.

Technological improvements over the years have made the fishermen's work easier, although even today it is a difficult job. Bob Bodi and Martin Hosko echo Keller's sentiments about the changes in the work.

BB: Well, it's like you say. The nets, there's no comparison with the improvement of the net, and even treating it, we used to just use pure tar, and when it was cold weather, the tar would get so heavy, a lot of times, you would have to knock the head off of the barrel. They come bigger than the barrels. So that changed. Everything down the line has improved tremendously. The pullers on the boats, we didn't used to know what a puller was on a boat. We used to pull it all hand over hand, and the "niggerheads" on the boats. . . . We didn't know what a "niggerhead" was. When we started, we hand over handed them up. Then we got a winch on the back, you crank. That was a great improvement.

MH: But what he's talking. See, that was when men were doing it. Crank it and you had to put the wraps on and you had to keep pulling, and when you wanted to get another hoop on the line here, you had to rest the crank against you or me. And don't let go of it cause it would come around and pow, take you right back in the neck.

BB: Everything in boats is improved in size, which is a good thing. Of course, you can fish in commercial fishing, you can get them too big, too. But the boats that Martin had, I think they was about just a nice size.

MH: Decked over boats is nice.

BB: They would carry a nice load. You could lay under a net good when you was scooping fish out. It was about a four ton, and else it was a hurricane, you was all right, you know. Pretty good shape. So everything from the time I started until now is much different as night and day.

Alva Snell remembered the long hours out on the lake and told two stories that contrasted the old with the new and the fisherman's hours with those of other occupations.

Now like, well I stopped around there at the barber shop, you know. Stopped in there to see if there was any news. You know, the barber always knows if there is any news cause everybody comes in and tells him. I was in there one day, and one fellow was complaining about, you know, working so damn hard. Eight hours a day and five days a week. I said, "Well God, I've got the record where I can show you where I would work from Labor Day to

Thanksgiving and not have a day off, which was seven days a week when you was fishing, you worked seven days a week." And I can remember getting home for Thanksgiving dinner one time at ten. That's the way you worked then, you know. If you were fishing, you had to make it while the fish were around. We didn't take any days off. We was there.

Tell you another funny thing that happened, you know. Years ago, as I told you, you worked seven days a week, and there was no eight-hour day like there is now. In fact, I joined what they called the trap-netters union at one time. There was lots of fishermen at that time, and the contract called for ten-hour days, eleven hours in the spring and fall when you was setting and pulling the nets, to get them out of the lake or something. But you worked ten-hour days and didn't think anything of it. Finally, got to a nine-hour day. Finally, down to eight. Well, I was out in the lake and just started with an eight-hour day, and looked at my watch, and said, "Oh my gosh, the day is, we gotta get started for home. We're going to be working overtime." And one of the fellows said, "I've never seen anything like it." He says, "I can stand on my head eight hours." Other fellow in the boat says, "Why, I can hold my breath for that long." It seemed so short after working for ten hours to work for eight.

The first story indicates that fishing is harder than other jobs, and the second that fishing in the past was harder than today. Notice the pride exhibited by Snell in these stories. The work was hard, but the men were up to it. This is a significant element in maintaining occupational identity after retirement: the retired fisherman can still see himself as a fisherman because from his perspective the ones fishing today are not fishermen in the same sense that he was. Their jobs are easier, and they do not work as hard. Every time Alva Snell tells these stories he is projecting and reinforcing his occupational identity.

Bob Bodi directly expressed the idea that fishermen in the past were superior.

There's no good fishermen anymore. After I quit, I know them all. Down there and setting their nets, same amount of men he did here. . . . And he'd tell that fellow that was working for him we done that, and he'd pretty near call Martin a liar. When they went out to pull, they pulled four nets, and they thought they did an awful big day's work. Now, Martin and I, we could go out, and Dick, and pull four nets, and we could be in here by eleven and going home. That's just the difference in the men. They was for what money they could get out of it. Not our kind of fishermen. We did it cause we liked it. And it wasn't the best paying job in the world, but it was far better than a lot of them.

At least one younger fisherman, Frank Reynolds of Toledo, agreed with the retired fishermen on this point. He had his own way of characterizing the technological and human changes in the occupation: ". . . the fishing has changed. The fishing here has changed. The methods and the boats we use. The old days, we had the wooden boats and the iron men. Now we got iron boats and wooden men."

The larger concept of a "golden age" of commercial fishing on Lake Erie is at work here; this was a time when men braved the elements out of dedication to their jobs. There are several other facets to this "golden age" image, one of which is the purity of the water in bygone days. Alva Snell and Chester Jackson recalled the same detail to illustrate the quality of water.

AS: Now that's another thing, when I started fishing, if you wanted a drink of water, you had a coffee can with a string on it, and just throw it overboard and had a drink. That's all there was to it. We drank right out of the lake, and didn't think anything of it. Then World War II, and then you didn't want to get it splashed in your eyes, cause it would make your eyes sore. You know, it got that bad.

CJ: When I started, we didn't carry no drinking water. You had a can, a tin can with a string on it. You wanted a drink of water, you dipped it over and drank it. Can't do that today. Those chemicals in there would kill you.

Another part of the image is the former bounty of the lake. One might think that fishermen would have become accustomed to abundant catches, but in describing certain experiences a note of wonder still came into their voices. Lewis Keller marveled at the variety of marine life they used to catch and contrasted that to present conditions.

By God, here in Sandusky today, I can remember the time when there used to be snails, big snails like that, and we used to get so many snails in the sand that we couldn't hardly get the seine to shore, and clams, clams would be hanging all over the seine when they pick them up in the sand and mud and that. Today you don't see a snail; you don't see a clam no more. That's the reason why there isn't no fish. All there is is junk fish like carp, sheephead, sowbellies. That's what they're getting in their seines today. The seine haulers are practically out of business today because they can't catch enough good fish to keep them going.

Martin Hosko recalls a particularly striking instance of both clear water and abundant fish in the past.

We used to wonder where the blue pike go in May and June. In June we would lose them. We used to wonder where the hell they would go. But this was in July, after 4th of July. Jerry [Martin's son] was just a kid about fourteen years old, and we'd run off a bunch, we'd run off of ten nets, and we were ready to eat dinner, so we set down to eat; it was dinnertime. And Jerry had a bottle of Coke and he opened it up, and threw the cap overboard, and I'm watching that cap, take another bite, eating you know, and I still see that cap. Water was so clear, and my God, how far can I see that cap down there? And I throwed something else over-board, and going down, and pretty soon I see a bunch of fish down there, and I seen blue pike so thick, just like a real thick school of minnows, blue pike, about ten feet down, but the water was clear. Now you could see distinctly, nice and blue, you know. And just as wide. So a couple of days later we lifted the nets, and we had a couple boxes like that, about three hundred pounds to a net of blue pike. Then we got a little shake up out of the east, and we got ten boxes. Those fish were there all the time on top of the water feeding on bugs.

This particular story has been passed on to a younger fisherman: Frank Reynolds recounts the same incident as part of his second-hand recollections of abundance in the days before he began fishing in the 1960s.

A common observation among older fishermen concerned the abundance of valuable fish for commercial purposes. Lewis Keller recalled an incident in which a storm prevented fishermen from emptying their nets, with the result that a great number of perch died in the nets.

I have seen the time, this is no kidding, and I'll tell you and I know it to be true, because I seen it with my own eyes. I've seen dead perch in that lake as far as you could see down the lake anyway. I don't give a damn which way you look, solid perch, dead. That's when we hit them down off of Cedar Point there, and them nets were just full of perch. We had a three day northeaster, and I mean it blew those three days, too, and drowned all those fish in those nets. After they are drowned, they are no good, see? We got out there after that blow, and all we did was just bail fish overboard. There weren't any live ones in it. Just tons and tons and tons of them. You wouldn't believe this unless you seen it, which I've seen with my own eyes.

Chester Jackson said that in the 1960s there were more perch being caught than could be sold and painted a vivid image of their numbers.

In the sixties there were so many perch out there. I made the statement one time, and the guy said, "You're crazy." I said, "There ought to be a million ton of perch in that lake." We had trap nets; these are trap nets. We had forty nets set out there, and every one of them had two or three ton of perch in them. We went out one day and couldn't pull them. We lifted them up, cut the top off, and let them go. You would lift the net up, and it wouldn't get off the bottom hardly and it would just boil like you've seen the freighter how it boiled and that. That's the way; the water would be all boiling when you'd bring it up. It was just loaded.

The abundance of fish meant a thriving fishing industry with more boats and nets. Lewis Keller emphasized the number of nets. "In the fall of the year, we used to have so many nets around Kelleys Island in that fall of the year you could pert near walk from one net to the next all around the whole island."

Part of the "golden age" image was the lack of governmental restrictions on fishing. We asked Bob Bodi about this.

PM: What was it like when you first started out fishing, Mr. Bodi? Were there game wardens?
BB: Didn't know what a game warden was then.
PM: Didn't have any?
BB: I never seen, all the while I ever fished, I only seen two game wardens down the creek in all my life.

No government interference, clear water, and an abundance of fish suggest that the "golden age" was a paradise compared with conditions today. This theme of nature as paradise is widespread in American culture and finds folk expression in tall tales, ballads, and legends (Boatright 1961; Dorson 1959; Mullen 1978b), and literary expression in such works as Twain's *Adventures of Huckleberry Finn*, Thoreau's *Walden*, and Hemingway's *The Sun Also Rises*, to name a few (Tanner 1965). In the retired fishermen's stories, the image changes somewhat to become paradise lost. That change may be indicative of a larger cultural shift of ideas, or perhaps it says more about the way many retired people view the past. All of the retired fishermen seem to yearn for earlier times, but they are able to keep those times alive through their imaginations and their stories about the past.

The image of the past in the minds of retired fishermen is not entirely positive, though; rather it is ambivalent, a mixture of "golden age" ideals with a recognition of the realities of hard work and long hours. Their starting-out stories emphasize family tradition, beginning work at a young age, and their early love of the water and fishing. The family connection is carried on for some men in their accounts of fishing on Lake Erie in their father's and grandfather's time. Even in the incidents that stress how difficult the work was, there is a sense of the fishermen's deep emotional attachments to their chosen occupation. In the stories about pure water and abundant fish, the fishermen project some of the ideals that gave them such a strong involvement with fishing, not just as an occupation but as a way of life.

3

Heroes, Characters, and Notable Men

Ed Lampe was an old-timer who fished out of Vermilion into the 1920s; he was known locally as an experimenter with fishing techniques and boats and as an extremely strong man. George Wakefield of Vermilion, who was not a fisherman himself but who knew most of the fishermen in the area, remembered some of the stories about Ed Lampe.

> Ed Lampe was the great big fellow, six feet six inches I would say. Rough and rugged as Abe Lincoln. In fact, I think he was a relative of Abe's. . . . And he walked just like Abe Lincoln, his hands were like that. Big guy. He was an unusual innovator, tried everything. Lost his pants on almost everything, but he made money at times when the fishing was good. He bought out the [names several boats]. She was the only steamer that was made that way. The others were conventional or inboard stern, smaller types. But Ed Lampe was a steel of a tug, conventional or otherwise.

Ed Lampe has all of the characteristics of an occupational hero, in this case the strongman hero as was Dick Kientz of Toledo, but the strongman hero is just one of several types of men that fishermen tell stories about. Another type is the local character, the eccentric who breaks the norms of society; Jib Snyder of Vermilion is the subject of a cycle of local character anecdotes. Then there were men who combined heroic and local character traits, such as John Lay who owned Lay Brothers Fishery in Sandusky and Clifford Baker (not his real name) who was a notorious rumrunner during Prohibition. The stories about heroes, characters, and notable men reveal a range of characteristics associated with commercial fishermen, from the worst to the best. They contain a mixture of esoteric (how fishermen see themselves) and exoteric (how they think others see them) images that project a complex occupational identity.

Ed Lampe as a hero to fishermen exemplified the importance of physical strength in the occupation. Chester Jackson recalled Ed Lampe's size.

> He was really a brute of a man. . . . Oh God, in his prime, I don't know what he was, but when I worked for him, he must have weighed two-twenty, two-thirty. He was hunched over then, and hell, he was still about six feet two inches. I suppose he must have been six feet six inches when he was in his prime. I mean his arms—he was a big man.

His physical attributes, mentioned by both Jackson and Wakefield and by every other person who knew of him, are obviously admired by fishermen. Lifting heavy nets by hand in the old days required great strength, and Ed Lampe was the ideal fisherman in this regard. One particular story about his strength was told by three different people; Alva Snell's version is the most detailed.

> They tell me he used to get leads for gill nets, you know, about that long [six inches] and big around as your thumb, you know, weighed about a pound, pound and a quarter, two pounds or something like that, depending on what you want. Well, anyway, they would come in boxes when they would buy them, you know. They said he was going up the street here one day with a box under his arm. He stopped to talk to somebody. He stood there about five minutes talking with them, and finally said, "Well, I guess I better go along. This thing is getting kind of heavy." Weighed two hundred fifty pounds. That's what the box weighed. He was standing there with it under his arm talking.

Jackson and Wakefield heard it in slightly different versions.

CJ: He was a working fool. Used to tell the story about him having two big five-gallon buckets of leads. That's what they used on the bottom in gill nets. Now we're talking over two hundred a bucket. He'd stand there talking, hanging onto both buckets. He was a big dude of a man.

GW: I heard that story this way, that he picked up a box of leads that nobody else would pick up; he would put it on his back like

this, walked across the bridge, the old bridge down there, and
another guy started talking—two hundred pounds on his back.
Funny.

According to Wakefield, Ed Lampe was somewhat disdainful of
other men's weakness.

Yes, I can tell you a few stories about Ed's strength. There are
many others, but one was a fellow named of Johnny Hoskins, they
used to fish a small mesh net, which was illegal, but he brought
the fish in. But he never brought the nets in. He would put the
nets in a box, put another box on the top and tie them up, and
then put them over the side with an anchor in the Erie Bay before
he came in so he wouldn't get caught with illegal nets. And that
was a hell of a lift up, and Ed would see the other guys trying to
heist it up there, and he would say, "What's the matter with you
fellows? Haven't you had your Wheaties today?" This was 1925
when Wheaties first come. But that's a story about Ed and his
strength.

He did not use his strength against other men unless provoked.
Snell told of a time Lampe used ingenuity and force to defeat a gang
of men.

Another time they tell he was either going or coming from down
the other end of the lake someplace. Years ago, trains, you know,
didn't run as fast as they do today. It was no trouble to hop a train
to go someplace. Back when I was a kid, I would hop a train to
town. That was nothing. They went slow and you would jump off.
Well, anyway, he was going someplace and hopped on this boxcar
that was open. When it lightened up in the morning, well, here's
three or four fellows on the other end all asleep. Of course, he
was all alone. They made out they was going to rob him. They
started talking pretty rough. He went back in one end. They kept
getting closer to him, and finally he started to run for the other
end, and as he went past the open door, he run and grabbed one
of them and throwed him out the door, and run to the other end
of the boxcar. And he run for the other end, and going past, he
knocked one out of the door. When he got them down to about
two, they decided to leave him alone. Oh, yes, he was a tough one.

This series of stories about Ed Lampe places him in a larger tradition
of American occupational strongman heroes. George Wakefield di-

rectly compares Lampe with Abraham Lincoln, bringing to mind the railsplitter image in the Lincoln legend; they both exemplify the American value of hard work. Like John Henry, whose strength enabled him to win a contest with a machine designed to do the work of many men, Lampe is described as having almost superhuman strength. Lampe can also be compared to Mike Fink and especially to Barney Beal, the strongman hero of Maine fishermen (Dorson 1959, 1964). The fight story told by Alva Snell places Ed Lampe in the tradition of Fink, the Mississippi River boatman who was known as a great brawler, and that of Beal, who was always the winner in his many fights. Maine fishermen tell several stories about Beal's amazing lifting power, stories that are similar to the story of Lampe casually holding the lead weights. Lampe, Henry, and Beal are also alike in that they fought or competed with outsiders, not men from their own community, and thus act as symbolic representatives of their group, creating in-group identity and establishing boundaries with other groups. Ed Lampe represents the most positive image of the working fisherman.

One other trait besides strength that everyone associates with Ed Lampe was his penchant for failed experiments. He put a car engine in a boat once and rigged some belts to it in order to drive the boat; but he ran into problems, as Snell recounts.

Well, he was out in the lake one time, and it got pretty rough. And got a little water in the boat, and he didn't stop to bail it out, and of course, a little oil always in the bottom of fish boats, you know. Got splashing up on his belts and first thing you know, the belts get slippery and he couldn't run. That's one of the things they tell about him trying his new tricks. And then he had this one boat, what was the name of that one now . . . anyway, he was fishing down the lake quite aways, and got ready to go home, and now let's see, I want to get this right. And he run a little ways, and he says, it was blowing strong from the west, and he says, "Guess we better anchor here," he says, "so it dries out." So they throwed over the anchor and laid there, and they said the boat was made out of sheet metal of some sort, kind of thin. He didn't make it too sturdy, you know, and everything they would go up on the seal, boy, they said they would come down and it would shake, you know. Finally, he says, kept blowing harder, and he says, "I guess we're going to have to go home anyway. Better pull the anchor." So they said they pulled the anchor, run all the rest of the night, and when it lightened up in the morning, they was right in the same place they was the night before. He was running all night long, but he wasn't going ahead any.

He also tried to dredge and haul sand out of the lake, but that failed too, according to Jackson.

He'd tackle anything, you know. He'd make a few bucks, and he was an experimenter all the time. But that sandsucker you got the big picture of went on the beach there east of Lorain. The guy at night, the harbor lights went out or something, and it was foggy, I guess. And the guy was tooting his horn. He thought it was somebody on the harbor, and hell, he went right up on the beach. That put him out of business. Then he went back fishing. That guy made two or three fortunes. That was a homemade boat he made. See, there was big sand grounds out here about seven miles. They would carry sand. They would come down here from Toledo to get it, from Sandusky.

The stories about Ed Lampe's failures are ambivalent: Snell and Jackson admire his ingenuity and the fact that he "made two or three fortunes," but they laugh at the times he failed and at times exaggerate his failures toward tall-tale status. Commercial fishermen, especially the older ones, are essentially conservative about their occupation; they believe in the "tried and true" ways of doing things and do not like to take risks with untried methods. At the same time, their work often calls for spur-of-the-moment innovation; they also value the ability to improvise a quick solution to a new problem. They recognize that changes in both technology and traditional procedures can be beneficial to them and that an experimenter such as Lampe is needed to try out new methods. If they work, then the other fishermen will adopt them. Ed Lampe, then, is a complex occupational hero, representative of at least two facets of the fisherman character: as a strongman he is entirely positive, as an experimenter he is an ambivalent figure.

Toledo had a strongman fisherman, Dick Kientz, although there were not as many stories about him as were told about Ed Lampe. Martin Hosko and Bob Bodi worked with Dick Kientz and remembered his strength.

BB: I'd call him a strong man, that Dick. I'd call him a powerful man, but he was good natured. . . .
MH: Nobody monkeyed with him. He was strong, but he was

like Bob says, good natured. . . . He learned to run a boat quicker than anybody I ever seen. He learned to repair nets quicker than anybody I've ever seen. Isn't that right, Bob?

BB: Yes.

MH: We'd be running off twine, you know, and that would be hard coming off backwards. You had to, it would be stuck on a pile of twine there, so you would have to pick up about one hundred, two hundred pounds of this chain, twine, and you would have to pull it loose. It would be stuck on the pile. Pull it lose, and it would take, poor Arthur, my brother-in-law, he couldn't pick up half one, one-fourth what Dick could. He would be on the other side lifting, jerking, you know, and that thing wouldn't be coming, and Dick he grabs his and gives it a yank, and break it loose, take it to the back of the boat, throw it overboard like he had ten pounds in his hand. He'd have maybe one hundred fifty pounds. He jumped and helped Arthur loosen it up, you know. Arthur says, "I don't know where you get the strength," he'd say to Dick. But Dick just like—he was all man, wasn't he, Bob? He made that hard work look so easy, you know. Poor Art, he says, "I don't know how you do it so easy." Strength.

Like Ed Lampe, Dick Kientz was remembered for more than his strength; intelligence was an important part of his character. Lampe was mechanically ingenious even though some of his experiments failed, and Kientz was a quick learner. The fishermen who talk about them want to emphasize that commercial fishing requires more than brute strength; intelligence is also necessary to succeed in the business. Another important trait for Kientz was his "good nature"; his strength was used for work and not for fighting. There is also an element of wish fulfillment in the Dick Kientz story: "He made that hard work look so easy." Every fisherman should have such great strength. The heroes and characters who fishermen choose to tell stories about reflect some of their own self-image. Ed Lampe and Dick Keintz are mainly positive sides of that self-image, but some characters embody the negative side.

One eccentric character, Jib Snyder, is still remembered by people in Vermilion. George Wakefield knew several stories about him.

Knew him very well. I slept with him once. Nobody else in town did that. I was a little kid, and I was interested in engines, and I kept his little boat, the "John L." or "John N." She had a two-cycle [engine] little son-of-a-gun without any mufflers, and she was hard to start, but I could start them all. Jib couldn't do a damn thing, so he wanted to go to the islands and I took him out, and we slept together in Middle Bass House. I could tell you one thing about Jib Snyder that I never tell anybody is that he drank a lot of wine on that trip. Hell, he got sick at night, and got up and opened the window and put his [butt] out there and let it go, right down the side of the house. He was sick at both ends, I guess. He was the dirtiest old son-of-a-gun, but I hung around him because he had engines. That's the reason I was helping him. I'd be late to school because I was starting his engines when he got on the lake. He was a filthy old fellow. He sailed as a cook on a schooner, an old timer, and an old fisherman, but he never caught any fish. He'd bring a couple of fish and he had old nets, and they weren't any good, and an old boat, "The Owl." . . . I can still see him sitting in the bottom of the boat. Couldn't see him. He'd be down there trying to start the damn engine. He'd go like this, and you would see the boat go like this, and Jib was rolling. One day he couldn't get in, so a tug pulled him, and stuff like that. . . . Jib he was drunk all the time. He was uptown. He was the river comedian in a way, and the Lighthouser boat would go by, and Vern Light- houser and Jack Lighthouser would all say, "I quit; I quit" when they went by Jib. Now they were kidding him. And Jib would say, "Those devils—those damn fools." Here's how that started. Jib was packing ice one day down at the Kishman [fish] house on the river, and Phil was the house man; he was the boss. He told Jib to go down and help those guys. They were bottlenecked in the ice flow. He wouldn't go down. He wanted to stay where it was dry on the seat, I guess or something. And Phil came back and said, "Jib, get down there." He wouldn't go. He said, "I quit" rather than go down there. That's where they got that big joke about Jib. "I quit." They would always say it in a strange voice, "I quit, I quit."

Mrs. W: Jib had a funny voice.

GW: Yes, he did. He had a funny voice.

Jib Snyder was a deviant, a filthy alcoholic who became the subject of stories told by townspeople and commercial fishermen. These local character anecdotes (Dorson 1968; Mullen 1978b; Stahl 1975) concen- trate on those traits that make him different: his alcoholism, his filthy habits, his funny voice, and his inability to interact with normal society. To the townspeople he is representative of all commercial fishermen, who they view as unclean, heavy drinkers. The fishermen recognize that the townspeople see them in this way and that Jib Snyder projects the negative stereotype, but they still tell stories about him. Storytelling is their way of dealing with some of the stereotypes. By telling stories about Jib, they can distance themselves from him by laughing at his eccentricities, implicitly making the point, "I'm not like that." George Wakefield, who is not a fisherman, tells stories that emphasize Jib's negative qualities more than do the stories fishermen tell. His stories contain the disgusting details of Snyder's behavior that fishermen do not mention, but Wakefield and the fishermen all see Jib Snyder as the "river comedian" whose antics are laughable.

The extreme negative and positive views of fishermen can be seen in a story Wakefield and others tell in which Jib Snyder and Ed Lampe are both characters.

Well, that's a story I've told about Jib and Ed Lampe. They used to have, they called it the hoosegow, the jail down across from Wagner's Hotel where Ray [Full]'s office is today, but the fish house is beside the street there. And Jib was in the jail. He was drunk and they locked him up. Old Luke McQueen locked him up, one of the constables, and he was rattling the door trying to get the hell out, and Ed Lampe came in with his sailing fisherman. This was back before he had his steam tug. When he first came to Vermilion, it was a cold night and he came in and tied up at the Kishman dock in black pitch night. Ed started ambling up the hill and he heard this rattling of the darn door, and he went over and he thought the guy wanted to get out, so he let him out. He was in the jail, so when he got up to the saloon, he heard about it and realized he had been a [prisoner].

Chester Jackson and his friend Percy Holl, a retired fish house manager, recalled this same story, but they said that Ed Lampe tore the door off the jail, which is in keeping with Lampe's strongman image. The hero and the local character interact in the same story, and both are true to their types. Ed Lampe uses his strength for what he thinks is a good deed, and Jib Snyder is in jail for drunkenness thus fulfilling the negative stereotype of fishermen as alcoholics.

Alva Snell mentioned that "Jib" was a nickname, short for giblets, and that once a year Dr. Dickson took Jib to the hospital for a bath. "He would say, 'Gee,' he said, 'those nurses' hands were so soft to clean him up.' " Snell also told two stories about Jib as a fisherman.

Now, let me see, was it Jib who was fishing for catfish, and he had it on the bottom of the boat, and he was rowing and one of the oars came out, and he fell over back, and he had an oar right in the middle of his back, and he couldn't get it out, you know. Couldn't reach it. Darn, had to come on in. He was fishing, and he just had this little boat, you know, and he was fishing all alone in it. He would fish for whatever was the best fish at the time, you know. Catfish or he would fish for herring or whatever happened to be around. And laughing one day, he says he was getting two cents a pound for herring at the time, and old Henry Kishman, the old fish company there years ago, says, tells the house foreman there, he says, "Tell so and so can't take his fish for awhile. The son-of-a-bitch is gonna get rich." Two cents a pound. I had a grandmother that lived on the lake bank down here beside of Fairport, and he used to go in no more than a rowboat. He'd go from here and row down there to Fairport, sixty or seventy miles. Fish down there for awhile and then come back.

Alva Snell's stories about Jib Snyder are not nearly as negative as those of George Wakefield. Snell emphasizes him as a comic figure who is not a good fishermen but who still works hard at it, rowing sixty miles to fish. Wakefield's view of Snyder was that he did not like to work. The same man is presented in different ways depending on who is telling the story. Snell feels a certain obligation to maintain a more positive image of fishermen, which Wakefield, not a fisherman, does not share.

The stereotype of Jib Snyder as a dirty, smelly drinker has been cleaned up by the townspeople of Vermilion as the town has become less of a commercial fishing port and more of a tourist center. There is now an arts and crafts boutique called "Old Jib's Corner" that has a clean well-dressed statue of Jib Snyder out front that bears little resemblance to the man Chester Jackson described.

That's the one, "Old Jib's Corner" up here, they named after him. He was an old river rat; he'd run a trot line, gill net. He never would take a bath. I don't think he was ever married, was he? Old bachelor . . . but that was named after him because he was probably one of the oldest fishermen anybody could recollect here in Vermilion at the time this opened up. But he was dirty. Oh, stink! You could smell him a block away.

Jib Snyder has become so well known that an article was written about him in *Ohio Magazine* in which are mentioned the store named after him and how the townspeople took care of him in his declining years (Scrivo 1986).

On the opposite end of the social scale from Jib Snyder was John Lay, who owned Lay Brothers Fishery in Sandusky; despite his status, he was also considered a character by the men who worked for him. Lewis Keller has a vivid image of "Old John" Lay even after fifty years.

Lay Brothers at one time was the largest independent fishery in the world, not just the United States, in the world, at that time. They had fisheries in Port Clinton. "Old John" Lay, he was still living yet when I was fishing for them, and he was an old rascal. He was a son-of-a-gun to work for, and he'd be down there every morning to see that the boys all got there on time, and got out on the boats all right, and boy, if you were a little late, he'd give you a dirty look, you know, but I always had trouble getting up in the morning. That was my biggest trouble when I was young, you know. I liked to sleep. They used to have to send a man up to get me out of bed pert near every morning, but by golly, I got by with them pretty good. We used to go out on these boats, you know, every day regardless of weather. Hell, if it was blowing, you'd go out anyway. "Try it." That was "Old John" Lay's saying. It might not be as bad as you think it is, you know?

He was a character, that guy. God damn, he was good hearted. He was just as tough as he was good. If he liked you, he liked you. If he didn't like you, he didn't like you, period. I don't know whether I told you. Years ago, when my dad was fishing for them years ago, and they used to furnish their breakfast for them. And they used to have a regular place upstairs in the fish house there where they had a regular breakfast where they could go in and eat, and old man Lay, "Old John," he used to sit at the end of the table every morning and look all his men over. And he'd see one of them wasn't eating, "How come you're not eating?" "Too sick." "If you're too sick to eat, you're too sick to go to work. Go back home." My dad used to tell me. He was a son-of-a-gun. . . . He was another that never believed in doctors. You never was sick; you just think you are, you know. If you was dying, you was just thinking you was dying. You wasn't supposed to be. But that's the kind of guy he was. He was quite an old rascal.

It would be a mistake to say that John Lay was a hero to the men who worked for him—his status removes him from their group sense—but he had many heroic traits that, when combined with some eccentric qualities, made him notable and worthy of stories. There is a note of pride in Lewis Keller's voice when he says that Lay Brothers was the biggest fishery in the world at that time. He clearly gives credit to John Lay's drive to succeed for this accomplishment, and as a worker he feels a sense of sharing in it.

In an occupation where hard work is valued, the owner and boss who works as hard as his men is admired. Carl "Darby" Barrington, an eighty-seven-year-old retired fisherman who worked for Lay Brothers, remembered how hard John Lay worked.

> He was rough, he was a hard . . . well, he knew what work was, that's how they got his, that's how the boys got the millions of dollars that they had. He worked. . . . We used to be leaving the docks by six o'clock in the morning, and he used to be there too, the old man. And Oscar Lay, the one son, he used to jump him too, once in awhile [laughter]. He was, he was, he was something.
>
> Before we had anything like that [power winches], you used to pull the nets all back out by hand on that big scow, he used to be right out there with you then too, and have ahold of that net pulling up, helping. And he was, he was no kid then yet already then neither. Yeah, he knew it; he knew what work was.

When the boss works alongside the men, then some of the barriers of class are broken down, and they can see him as being like them. They are more willing to work hard because he works hard.

He was rough and he was hard, but he was also "good hearted," as Lewis Keller said. The softer side of John Lay was also emphasized by Roy Shepherd, an eighty-four-year-old man who hauled fish from the islands to Sandusky for Lay Brothers before he retired.

> **PM:** What was John Lay like, what kind of a man was he?
> **RS:** Far as I'm concerned, wonderful. He and I used to have a lot of arguments and what have you but. . . . Well, he had a big Lincoln sedan, and pert near every morning they would start out with boxes and boxes [of fish], and drive all over Sandusky, and give fish to the poor people, and also those that weren't so poor got fish. But he really was, he did an awful lot. . . . Yeah, he was a character.

"Darby" Barrington mentioned the same charitable impulse in John Lay.

He used to take fish that happened to get in there that was under-sized, you know, that's what he would most generally would do then. They have to sort them out, you know, couldn't ship them out, and they put them in a cooler, and the next day he'd have one of the fellas working in the shanty wrap up a bunch of bundles, and he'd put them in his automobile go out and deliver [them to widows].

Perhaps an even more important trait in terms of the way his workers regarded him is that he was generous with them. "Darby" Barrington said:

There's a lot of times after you got fishing, got going, and the fish would hit sometimes, strike pretty good, you know, and you'd have a pretty good lift during the day. Lot of times, sometimes you'd go up, when you'd go up to eat, you know, everybody'd go up to eat, you know, and when you go into the dining room there, that day and get at the table, you know, all your plates was turned upside down, and when you turned your plate over there, there'd be an envelope under your plate, maybe with a five or a ten dollar bill in it, extra. But when the old man died, that was all, that was done.

It is unusual in American occupational folklore to find such positive stories about an owner and boss. Perhaps this is because in concentrating on heroes and characters folklorists have neglected to collect narratives about bosses, or perhaps it is because John Lay was a unique individual and that there were not many owners like him. His combination of toughness and generosity have kept him alive in the stories his workers continue to tell about him.

Throughout the western part of the lake, Clifford Baker's fishing skills, business acumen, boat-handling abilities, and stubborn conviction are spoken of with great respect. In the stories he told of himself and in those other fishermen tell of him, his work is usually described in superlatives: he had the fastest boats, the best designs, the best-treated employees, the cleanest and most sanitary fish house, and so on. Other area fishermen who tell stories about him also clearly admire the independence and roguishness in the face of authority that stood him well, particularly in the late 1920s, when he added to his fishing income by running liquor and beer across the lake from Canada to the United States. He became an outlaw hero during these years, and even after he quit rum-running, stories continued to be told about his exploits. Unlike most of the other notable fishermen about whom stories are told, Baker was still living at the time of our fieldwork. He openly discussed his illegal activities during Prohibition and seemed willing to have these stories published. After his death, his wife requested that we withhold his actual name, and we have respected her wishes. The name *Clifford Baker* is a pseudonym, and all of the personal and place names mentioned in his accounts are also fictitious.

Baker's navigational ability first brought him steady work running liquor. He tells his own version of the "starting-out" story:

> I was working for my brother for a dollar a day and my board. Then when we got married I got fifteen dollars a week, and that was in 1926 when I got married in April, and I went rum-running in the summer. I knew my wife was gonna have a baby, and I'm thinking, "Fifteen dollars a week, how in the hell am I gonna—?" Them days the wages was somewhere between fifteen dollars and twenty-five dollars a week. "How in the hell am I gonna support a wife and a kid?" When I got started there, there was a guy broke down off Rocky Point just a little ways this side of the Ontario River, and I was fishing for my brother in Barry Canal. And [this guy's] boat broke down, he had four hundred cases of beer and fifty cases of liquor on there. . . . He was looking for some fisherman to go tow it in, because he was going to Laketown going in the bay. So somebody sent him down to my brother's place. My brother wasn't home, so I'm in charge of the fishery for him. And there was one boat [available]; it was fifty-five foot long, big heavy-duty sixty horsepower motor, and you couldn't fish with that. And somebody sent him down. I said, "No, I won't go cause that boat don't belong to me." "Who owns that?" [he said]. I said, "Toledo Fish Company." He said, "Mike and Bill Collins?" "You mean Mike and Bill Collins?" I said, "Yeah." "Well," he said, "Mike Collins has got, I've got bottles of ale for him on that boat." He said, "He'll let you go." I said I wouldn't go unless I got a permission. Okay. So he drove me to Mike's and he got ahold of Mike's number. He's selling him stuff. So he got his number, he called him, and then [Mike] talked to me. This was about eleven-thirty at night. And he told me, "Well," he says, "I don't care if you take the boat, Cliff, but," he says, "if you happen to get caught, don't tell them I give you okay." I said, "Okay, Mike." So that's all I need. So I says, "Where's the boat?" He told me right off of Rocky Point.

Now I know where Rocky Point was, and I takes off for Rocky
Point about eleven-thirty that night. About five o'clock—the boat
I had going about eight, nine mile an hour—them days that's
about all a fish boat would run. So, break of day, by God, I saw a
low dark spot there and I'm heading right smack on his boat. And
he had one of his men on the boat with me so I didn't go alone.
I said, "That's the boat." I pull up right alongside of it. I throwed
my towline on and I towed it in. He was gonna give me a hundred
dollars. Now picture a man—picture yourself working for fifteen
dollars a week. One hundred dollars was looking at you. So I took
it right to the end of the pier and I got to the dock there, he's out
there with a rowboat. . . . "Cliff" [he said,] "way you know the
lake, you ain't got no business a-fishin'!" . . . "I want you to run a
boat for me. And you can make a trip every day, and I'll give you
one hundred dollars a trip. I got a good boat for you." So he come
back, he says, "I told you I give you one hundred dollars if you
get that boat for me." And he says, "My man tells me you went
right straight for that boat! Right where I told you to go!" He
says, "Anybody knows the lake like that ain't got no business
a-fishin'. I want you to go on a boat for me." And that's how I got
started rum-running.

Besides being a starting-out story, this narrative also attempts to
justify his getting involved in illegal activities. He starts the story by
mentioning what a low wage he was getting fishing and his need for
more money because his wife was having a baby. In the middle of
the story he appeals directly to his listener for understanding, "Now
picture a man—picture yourself working for fifteen dollars a week.
One hundred dollars was looking at you." He places the listener in his
position in order to justify his actions. The occupational hero element
he emphasizes here is his navigational ability; as we saw in chapter 1,
being able to find your way in the dark or in a fog was a highly prized
skill, and Clifford Baker was one of the best at doing this.

Even though Baker had a number of scrapes with the Coast Guard
and other law-enforcement officials, he regarded himself not as a
criminal, but as a person making good money by providing a service
to the public.

I don't care what business, how rotten it is, there's honesty even
amongst the thieves. I don't consider myself a thief. I never stole
anything, never done anybody any harm. And there was hundreds
of people tickled to death by what I done. . . . But I didn't have

to be ashamed for what I done. I didn't sell them. We brought
them. I was what you call a rumrunner. There was a difference
between rumrunners and bootleggers. Bootleggers was the ones
that run the place where they sold it. I just brought it. I got paid
for just hauling it across the lake.

Because, honestly, I never felt that I was doing anything wrong.
I wasn't stealing. I wasn't doing anybody any harm. I was making
a lot of friends. A lot of people admired me for this. They thought
I was something. I didn't do it just for that; I was doing it for
money. People just was tickled to death to get it.

His statements place him directly in the tradition of the American
outlaw hero, of Jesse James, Sam Bass, and "Pretty Boy" Floyd, who
break the law at least partially because people in the community do
not believe the law is right. Many people thought that Prohibition was
wrong and that they should be able to drink alcohol; Clifford Baker
made sure they could get it. The image of the outlaw has a great appeal
for commercial fishermen because they see many of the laws that
regulate their occupation as being unjust. Thus, it was appropriate
that Baker became a hero figure to fishermen.

In his stories of encounters with the Coast Guard while rum-running, Baker shows the hero in action.

I wasn't afraid of only God Almighty. I wasn't afraid of no law. . . .
And I hauled for three different groups. I had spots I would go
into there at night—number one, number two, so on spots. And
I never told you where I'm bringing a load for somebody else.
TL: You and I'd have our place and you and this other guy'd
have a place.
CB: Right. I tell you where I'm gonna be, and I tell you I be
there one o'clock, I'll be there one o'clock. I always allowed myself
a little extra time. If it was blowing pretty good, I liked it better
on a good dark night. I didn't have a ghost of a chance of the
Coast Guard seeing me—not a ghost of a chance. Of course,
nowadays we got all the radars and all that crap. But no, it was
sort of exciting, and I had Coast Guard take me twice out of
Canadian water, too.
TL: Oh, yes?
CB: Yeah. It's a lousy cheating when they take a man out of
Canadian water. They have no business there, thirty miles into
Canadian water. But they shot my boat and crippled my engine
and I was helpless. I had to give up. At that time I was right close

to the line and I stayed there all day. And if those guys would have testified for me in court that they took me out of Canadian water, cause they shot me up. And the skipper was afraid I was going to do that. I wanted him to take me in. Take me in. And he wouldn't. You know where he took me? Down here to Aurora you know where the ferry dock is there? And the dock was there and they run the Coast Guard [boat] alongside there, and they stuck the guns at me and my partner and made us get off the Coast Guard. Get off. Then he went back to Seagull [Island] and picked up the boat that he shot up. He left a man on the boat there. Now that's a crooked son-of-a-bitch if he was a Coast Guard, you see. But they was the law. I wasn't doing as much wrong as he was. They had no business in Canadian water. He shot my boat, took my boat away from me. I had rights to be in Canadian water. [My wife] said, "If I was you, I wouldn't brag about it," she said, "That's not nice." I said, "Honey, you don't know how many people I made happy." There was people—I could go in South Park in the Hungarian part of town there in Laketown them days, and I could go to any bootlegging joint and I couldn't buy a drink. Everybody thought I really was somebody.

Self-promotion is part of the American hero tradition; Davy Crockett built up his own legend through newspapers, an autobiography, and almanacs (Dorson 1959, 203–14), the oilfield hero Gib Morgan published a pamphlet about his own exploits (Dorson 1959, 228), and oral tellers of tall tales often make themselves the heroes of their tales (Mullen 1978b, 130–48). Clifford Baker follows in this tradition: he introduces his story of the arrest by the Coast Guard with, "I wasn't afraid of only God Almighty. I wasn't afraid of no law," and he ends it with, "Everybody thought I really was somebody." Several heroic traits emerge in this story: the fearlessness of the outlaw, the dirty tactics of his opponents, and the support he has from the community.

After five years in the business, Baker decided to return to fishing when the stakes became too high.

But then, finally, my partner says, "Clifford, I hear there's some damn hijacking from Chicago muscling in here." He says, "To-night I want you to," he had a La Salle automobile and he had a Cadillac. He says, "I want you to drive the La Salle." He said, "I'm gonna be prepared for hijacking." He's got a Thompson machine gun on his leg. I'm thinking, "Clifford Baker, what in the hell are you getting into?" That was out of my luck right there. I didn't say nothing to him that night, and nothing happened. Everything was fine, and the next day I says, "Tom, I'm quitting. I'm going fishing."

The hero who is to live to tell of his own exploits must know when to quit; the alternative is to die in a hail of bullets as Jesse James, Sam Bass, and Bonnie and Clyde did. Finally, Baker's identity as fisherman became paramount; the dangers were too great to continue in rum-running. He started his own business, which he built into one of the most successful fishing and fish-selling operations on the lake, known for its good business practices and clean conditions. The Baker Fish Company went out of business at the beginning of the current period of difficult times for the local industry, and Clifford Baker spent his retirement years until his death telling stories about his adventures to friends and family.

Other fishermen recount stories they have heard of Baker's exploits and accomplishments, including his storytelling abilities.

Sam Winston: I mentioned to you that it must have been somewhere in the early twenties he [Clifford Baker] was just starting to get into fishing, and rum-running got to be a big thing, and he got into that several years.
TL: He didn't say anything about that. He didn't bring that up.
SW: He'll tell you if you ask him. He'll tell you. Yes, he used to be a wizard on them old dark boats and putting them. . . . He was telling me about a month ago about a 1,300-cubic-inch engine he had. Two five-inch exhaust pipes for rum-running with no muffler. He said he could leave the shore here at Carson, and he would be over in Batesville in Canada, it's right here across the bridge, in thirty-seven minutes. And he would load up and he would make it here just in time for four or five minutes for the time to run over there. Big motor in that boat. He made quite a few trips, and they shot quite a few boats out from under him, and sunk him a couple times.

I think one time he was telling me about the U.S. Coast Guard was waiting for him at the line, and it was in the spring, and it was quiet and there was a lot of fog banks out there. Run so far and you would just disappear in them. And he could see a fog bank off in the ways, and he took off and he just got to it, and he said the bullets started bouncing off the water. He just got into the fog. He ran into the fog. He said he had a compass and he had a watch, and he ran in that fog for about twenty to twenty-five minutes and he had a location over there in Wyandot. . . . And he kept running, and he thought he was just about there, and he finally pulled out, slowed down, touched the bottom of the boat in a few feet of water. It was still foggy, and he just ran a little more, and the fog opened up, and there was the guy setting waiting for the stuff. And he ran over and he says, "Hurry up and unload this thing because they are right behind me someplace." So they unload it. . . .

Well, he knew the lighthouse was over there, and he pulled up and tied up there, and went to talk to the lighthouse man. He was only talking about four or five minutes, and here comes the Coast Guard right out of the fog, you know. They just asked him a few questions, you know. He said, "Oh, I've been setting here for a couple hours waiting for the fog to lift." They couldn't really identify him, but they were sure it was him. He didn't have nothing in the boat, you know, but the motor was hotter than hell. The lighthouse keeper says, "Clifford has been here for the last hour and half at least waiting for the fog to lift. He don't want to get lost going into shore." Hell, he only had a mile to go, and he just ran thirty miles. It was so quiet out there and there wasn't a ripple on the water. He was pretty sure what they were doing was following his bubbles, you know, in the fog. Cause he had done that himself already. Turn right around and follow his bubbles right back to shore at Bayport. But he's got a hundred stories like that.

This story projects several heroic traits: Baker's skill as a navigator, his use of the fastest boat on the lake, his fearlessness in dealing with the Coast Guard, his intelligence in outwitting them, and the community support in the form of the lighthouse keeper who lied to protect him. This is reminiscent of the legends in which Jesse James escaped a pursuing posse with the aid of helpful townspeople. Sam Winston's admiration for Clifford Baker in his illegal activities is clear.

Tom Carswell's discussion of Baker shows how fishermen continued to admire him even after he retired as an outlaw.

At one time I guess he [Clifford Baker] had a lot of money. When the Feds started cracking down so hard on them, and they started losing boats. They seized their boats. But he just about lost it. He had just enough money left, he bought a home, and he built twenty-one nets, and he built a boat, a fish boat. And that's how he got started in the fish business. It came from bootlegging. He can tell you stories about having machine-gun bullets just missing his head by a half inch.

TL: Well, yes, Sam [Winston] was telling some second-hand stories he had heard running in the fog all the way back across.

TC: I heard most of the stories at least twenty times. And they told it word for word the same every time, so that fog had to be—

TL: We had a great talk. We were there three hours. . . . They were saying he had a boat that had 1,300-cubic-inch engine in it.

TC: Yes, just blast across. He could be from Laketown to Batesville which is just across from Rivertown, south of Warwick thirty minutes.

TL: Yes, that's what I heard, thirty or thirty-five minutes, something like that.

TC: But when the government got onto them so bad, they were losing too much money. But back in that time, they would clear as high as $10,000 in one load. That's about like $100,000 today.

TL: Sure it is.

TC: And they all had four-inch valves in the bottom of the boat in case they would get too close, they could scuttle the boats. Boat load and all.

TL: Not just the load, but the whole thing.

TC: Whole thing. Think about the kind of engines Cliff run. But he is one of the best mechanics that I know, and he tuned his own boats. He had the fastest boats on the lake. He was one of the larger processors. Cliff caught lots of fish. He made lots of money. But he was a hard worker, and he had such a neat, clean operation.

TL: That's what everybody said, including him. . . . Everybody has mentioned that he really had a good operation.

TC: Yes, he did. He had a very, very clean operation. If the place smelled like fish, he was in orbit. It was very sanitary. There was no fish smell like you have in a fish house.

The same sort of image occurs here as in Winston's story—the outlaw hero with the fastest boat—but Carswell turns this into images of Baker's reputation as a fisherman—the best equipment, hardest worker, the cleanest operation. The outlaw image merges with the commercial fisherman image, indicating that the identities are not that far apart.

Notable fishermen who were thought of as characters by other men in the industry could come from any part of the social scale and could reflect both positive and negative images, at times in the same figure.

Ed Lampe and Dick Kientz had the valuable attribute of strength in an occupation that stresses physical labor, but they were also intelligent men who showed the mental side of good fishing. Jib Snyder embodied the negative stereotype of fishermen—alcoholic, dirty, and smelly—and he is viewed as a comic character, an exception to the clean, sober family men who make up the largest group of fishermen. John Lay was not a fisherman, but his traits of hard work and generosity as the owner of a fish company were admired by the men who worked for him. Clifford Baker speaks and is spoken of in terms of his hard work and high standards on shore and his skill and cunning on the lake, even when these abilities were developed and used in what were illegal activities at the time. Some of his recollections indicate his mixed feelings about his rum-running activities; for instance, his statement ". . .there's honesty even among the thieves. I don't consider myself a thief. I never stole anything . . ." and his distinction between rum-running and bootlegging. Nevertheless, the portrait he paints of his work at the time is positive: he is the "little guy" trying to make a living for his family during a difficult time, who was able to become "somebody" through his work. Especially during the occupation's present difficulties, other fishermen recite their versions of his stories as historical evidence for their portrayal of themselves as working men made outlaws in some sense by the times. In fact, all of these men are remembered through stories that also help to explain the present. The images of the past and characterizations of the present we now hear are created out of actual incidents filtered through the memories, imaginations, and ideals of the storytellers.

4

Hazards

Well, I just couldn't begin to tell you of all the times I've had fishing like that—close calls, many of them. I shook hands with St. Peter a lot of times.

Lewis Keller's statement about close calls could have been made by any of the fishermen we interviewed. Although commercial fishing trips on western Lake Erie rarely last more than a day, during which fishing boats are not too far from shore, fishing is still a dangerous occupation. Ice and other severe early and late season weather conditions, winds and storms that can come up quickly and can make the waters of such a shallow lake extremely rough, and dense fogs that can obscure the constant freighter traffic through shipping lanes all pose hazards for fishermen. Consequently, many of the stories fishermen tell are about narrow escapes.

Fishermen's stories about hazards they have faced function along with other occupational narratives as a means of projecting their identity. Other hazardous occupations also have narratives that function in similar ways; firefighters (McCarl 1985), coalminers (Green 1972), loggers (Toelken 1979), and oil-field workers (Boatright and Owens 1970) are just a few of the occupational groups with traditions of hazard narratives. For commercial fishermen, hazard stories provide a positive image; they may be frightened when they are caught in a bad storm, but they maintain control and finish the job at hand. An important part of their self-image is that they are outdoorsmen who are close to nature as part of their everyday experiences. The hazard stories show them interacting with nature at its most violent, but because an important appeal of the occupation is being in nature, they have to face these hazards directly. Only by having had close calls can they earn the right to be considered commercial fishermen in the deepest sense of that identity. The hazard stories show their pride in having faced danger and in having survived it.

Lewis Keller told about a summer storm that almost sank his boat.

I seen the time coming in along that jetty over there when the captain of the boat was Jess Bailey, and a northeaster, and I've always said as long as I've lived around the lake, that's the roughest spot in the whole Lake Erie is coming right in along that jetty going into Sandusky in a northeaster. I'm telling you, boy, I've never been so scared in my life. That's when we had one of these little thirty-six boats yet, and we was setting twine that day, and there were just the two of us in the boat. We were running anchors, boy, and it was picking up out of the northeast all day long. Down off of Cedar Point, down there aways, a northeaster it ain't too bad, you know, cause you could still set up twine and that, and it wouldn't be too bad, but, boy, when you came into that jetty by Sandusky and go along there, and man, I'm telling you, to look back there and see those waves, and they would look a mile high. They used to call them the three sisters. There would be one wave that wouldn't be so bad, the next one would be a little bit bigger. The third one was always the pits.

We were coming in, just the two of us in the boat, and in the summertime everyone was always blacker and healthier, and sunburnt because years ago you used to get so much twine dust, you'd get burnt so bad you'd look like a nigger, and anyway going in there that day, I seen that wave coming, and we had made two or three before that, and they didn't bother us, but we got on that third wave, and just as we got on the third wave, the boat just seemed like it stopped and that broke, and I'm telling you, water, both sides of the boat, boy, what I mean she just come in, and oh brother. I thought we sure as hell was gonna sink it. And you want to see somebody get out a handpump, you should have seen me. That's when we had them old handpumps, and Jesus Christ, you had to get it out quick because on those boats years ago, they used to have the engine up in front. They used to have a little four-cylinder engine in them, and they set so low in the boat, that if we hadn't pumped like hell to get that water, that water would have got up and killed that motor. You'd have been done for. That's all, and man, I'm telling you, I don't know, I looked at the guy running the boat and he looked at me. I don't know who was the whitest, him or me. I was scared. I've had a lot of close calls already in my life on boats and that, but that was the worst scare a guy ever had, and I was young yet at that time. Man, I never wanted to go through that again, I'll tell you that.

Like his starting-out story, this one is full of vivid details even though it took place many years ago, indicating the strong impression the incident made on him. He refers to himself as looking "like a nigger," and he was not the only fisherman to use racial epithets or such common terms as "niggerhead" for a piece of equipment on the boats. There are no black commercial fishermen on western Lake Erie, but the white fishermen do not seem any more racist than the general white population of the area. Keller is not prone to using exaggerated imagery in his stories, but in this one he invokes several strong images: the waves looked "a mile high," and the two men were so scared that they turned white through their deep suntans. He feels compelled to exaggerate in order to emphasize the intensity of the experience. He also used more exclamations than usual for the same reason: "boy," "I'm telling you," "Jesus Christ," and "oh brother." Also significant is his use of traditional knowledge about the lake, significantly couched in metaphoric terms: if he did not know about the "three sisters" before this experience, he definitely knew about them afterward. The implicit sexism of making the dangerous waves female is a traditional part of a culturally defined male occupation. This incident could be seen as an initiation ritual with some sexual connotations then; once he has gone through this danger in the lake as a young man, he can be fully accepted as a fisherman. Every time he tells the story, he re-creates the ritual.

Traditional knowledge is also imbedded in another of Keller's hazard stories.

PM: So even when the water was that choppy, you'd go out?
LK: Hell, yes. I was trying to tell you that day we went down to the elbow. That was summer fishing, see? We used to time ourselves from the jetty to your course. You would take your course out of the northeast, east, wherever you're going down there. Get your course on your compass. Then we'd run one and a half hours, and that was right to where they called the elbow. That's where your line [the border with Canada] runs down from Middle Island and then turns at the elbow and goes the other way. We

were getting a lot of blue pike down there that year. One and a half hours to get down there that day, and that same day it took us five and a half to come back home. That's how rough it was.

In both of his storm stories, the lake is seen as an enemy, an active force that has to be overcome in order to do the job. At the same time, the lake is the source of the fish that makes the job possible. Fishermen both love and fear the lake.

Riding heavy seas with a load of fish is one of the most dangerous situations because the boat is more likely to sink when waves wash over it. Lay Brothers fishing boats used to bring their catch into one of the Lake Erie islands, and then it would be hauled by another boat to Sandusky. "Darby" Barrington ran this boat back and forth, and he encountered some severe storms in his forty years of work.

> You see I was always all alone on that boat, and of course several times I came in there, and we used to have that deck, the deck would be filled with boxes of fish from the back of the cabin clean to the back end of the boat, maybe have a hundred and fifty to close to two hundred boxes of fish on there. And you were down in the water then, and I've hit a couple of storms coming in with them there. I used to have the front of the cabin, the front of the pilot house there was two little windows here on each side of the pilot house there, and that was, we used to stand there, and we used to have water as far, pert near a foot deep in front of my face where it'd come up over the bow of the boat and right down and up.

Chester Jackson and Alva Snell were together once with a boatload of fish when they almost sank. Jackson tells the story.

> That was the closest time I ever come to being sunk was right out here outside the Ford plant. Production was heavy, and we was under a net, and it took us an hour maybe to clean it out, and a northeaster come up. And I was loaded. I had about twelve or thirteen thousand pounds of fish on. My capacity on a flat day was only sixteen thousand five hundred or maybe seventeen thousand pounds. Alva Snell was on the back. This northeaster come up. I mean it was nice when we got under the net, and the longer we bailed trying to clean that net out, the bigger the seas got. Now, this Lake Erie in fifteen or twenty minutes, a northeaster can kick up one terrific swell. Well, Alva was on the stern cleaning his end out, and I was up on the bow with my other helper cleaning the

bow end of the net out. And I had the motor in reverse all the time to keep the net, the boat under the net. Had her going hard in reverse. And she kept—we was loaded. We had fish right to the gunnels. She took a big sea, a few hundred pounds of fish washed off. She took another one. She went right up into the engine room, and when that is up, over a ton of fish went right with it. I says, "Get the hell up here, Alva, and get out of here." We just run right out from under it. That's the closest I ever come. She wouldn't have took one more. She'd have sunk us right there. That's the closest I ever got to sunk. Once we got started, we still had about 11,000 pounds aboard, which is loaded right to the hilt. We had a hell of a time getting home. It was a northeaster tail wind. Those seas were really coming over.

In Jackson's and Barrington's stories, the lake almost wins the struggle. Barrington projects a sense that he faced this sort of danger often, and that he just kept going. In Jackson's case, he and Snell had to act quickly in order to avoid being sunk. In both stories, the image is of courageous fishermen confronted with life-threatening situations.

Fishermen do not often admit to being seasick, but Jackson told another story about seas so heavy that he was.

Captain Floro—it's a wonder Alva Snell didn't mention his name, but he was a brute. He wasn't as big a man, but he was—the water was never rough enough on Lake Erie to keep him in. I know in the forties. . . . So this was in December, and they had their nets out there, and it was iced in up here. So he got—see all these companies work together, two crews from here went down there, and this Captain Floro, he had a steamship, a steam tug, about an eighty footer. We went way down off of Cleveland, maybe two and a half, three hours out of Lorain. Oh, the seas were so high. It's the only time in my life I ever got seasick. We were pulling these nets. They were several nights out, and had some dead fish in them. These were gill nets now. . . . I set on the stool and go to haul the nets, picking them out, you know. I'd vomit. The seas would come in, wash it away, vomit again. I worked all day sicker than a dog. But those seas were so bad, that steamship'd get the water right over the side, wash everything aboard. That was bad. This guy, nothing would stop him. First, he had to get the boat under. This was a steel tug with steam, and he was a hell of a good captain. He knew what he was doing. He knew more than I did. That was the worst day I ever put in my life.

This story contains some elements of the hero legend: Captain Floro is the strongman determined to finish the job against overwhelming odds, but he is not foolish; as Jackson says, "He knew what he was doing." There is a contrast here between Floro who does not get seasick and Jackson who does. When one of us (Pat Mullen) went out on a gill-net tug and got seasick, the fishermen had a good time making fun of the novice, and seasickness is usually associated with an inexperienced person. Here Jackson, although an experienced fishermen, is not the equal of the heroic Captain Floro.

Retired fishermen are not the only ones who tell of being caught in bad storms; active fishermen also have their share of close call stories. While standing on Joe Herr's boat, Herr and Paul Leidorf both related harrowing experiences.

JH: See these new windows here?

PM: Yes.

JH: That's cause they was blowed out three years ago, two years ago.

PM: Completely blown out?

JH: Yes, I blew them out of that boat that we had in Canada two years ago, too, in a storm. Blowed it right out.

PL: I got caught in seventy mile an hour waves, and I had maybe six ton on there, and had to enter into it cause we were heading home. If you headed the other way, there would be pinches the other way. She was howling, but we come in with her. We checked her down good and that.

JH: You get cold when you gotta stand there and run that sucker when that wind's blowing about seventy miles an hour and that shit coming through the windows.

Leidorf's penchant for understatement came out in his description of weathering a one hundred mile per hour wind at sea.

I was loaded extra heavy. I put two fish nets on against the tail gate, and we went out and lifted two nets which was full. So I had the fish in the front, and pulled the two nets and run those two off, and it started storming, and started throwing a lot of water over the roof. Nets that was dry was washed in back, and I had to batten this boat down, pumps running. . . . Shut the cabin door, and I was still standing in water about that deep standing on top of the hatch. Thinking about putting your life jacket on, but didn't want to get anyone excited. It was a thunderstorm they had predicted, but we figured it would blow ten minutes and be over with, you know. Well, she blowed an hour. . . . That's the only time that I can ever say that I was on this boat and I thought I might get water in my back pockets.

The active fishermen share an occupational self-image with the retired ones: they have all had to face the risk of sinking and drowning during heavy seas, and they have all faced it directly and survived. If anything, the active fishermen are more matter-of-fact about the dangers: Leidorf's understatement is in contrast to the dramatic imagery of Keller. Retired fishermen tell stories to relive adventures they faced twenty years ago; active fishermen must go out the next day to face possible dangers.

Because fishermen are pulling in nets early in the spring and late in the fall, they often must contend with freezing conditions. Chester Jackson described working with frozen gloves.

PM: What about fishing in cold weather?

CJ: That's rough. You get ice. I've fished out there and had ice on my gloves, freeze right on your gloves. You had to wear cotton gloves, but if you get your blood circulating, you're all right. That's where, but if you stand around, you gotta circulate your blood. Oh, it's cold, that ice. . . .

PM: Can you remember any particular times when the cold weather was extremely bad?

CJ: Well, we got caught with our nets out here. That was in the 50s, no it was in the 60s. Worked for Kishman at the time. Didn't get our nets pulled out. We had a real cold spell. We had to break the ice up and down the line of nets before we could start pulling them. So much ice there was six or eight inches thick. That was the coldest I ever pulled out.

Lewis Keller told of similar cold weather experiences.

It used to be rough, but in the winter months and the fall of the year when we used to fish them whitefish nets over there in the fall of the year, and man, you get over there, and your hands were cold and your gloves would freeze on your hands. Well, it was rough. . . . Then when it came to pulling the twine, boy it would be so damned cold, that you'd take and try to pull the net, the net would freeze faster than you could pile it up. It would be just like piling up wire.

My wife could even tell you, hell, I would come home. Hell,

you'd have your oil hat on and your oil coat and everything, hell, would be solid ice. Your gloves would freeze to your fingers, and your gloves would be froze stiff, but your hands wouldn't be cold though. Cause once you get your gloves wet, and once you get your hands warm in them, then you're working like that, they'll stay warm. But your [face] will freeze harder than hell. Oh, I've put some cold days in. That's the hell of it.

As Alva Snell showed us a photograph of a boat covered with ice, it reminded him of a story.

That particular picture I showed you of that boat here. That's on the twenty-second of December. We were iced down. You can see the ice in the boat if you look close. That's why they come and took the picture. See the ice all over it? Well, we didn't get our nets till the fifteenth which is the end of the season. . . . You know, went out on the twenty-second of December, and we didn't get in till two in the morning. They had turned the pier lights off and the other lights, and it come up a snowstorm, a blizzard, and we couldn't see to get in. Well, when we got in, they was pretty worried about us, and sent the photographer down to take a picture of us all iced up. That's the reason I got that particular picture.

Snell, Keller, and Jackson had similar memories of working in icy conditions: an already difficult job becomes even more difficult. The fisherman toughened by hard work in the summer had to become even tougher in the winter. Their personal stories project an image of men hardened by their constant exposure to the extremes of nature.

The storytellers have survived their personal encounters with winter conditions, but they told stories about boats and men that did not. Alva Snell told the following.

And, oh yes, there are lots of stories. I remember one time a couple boats, I think from Ashtabula, they were coming up here to lay up in the fall of the year, so they would be ready in the spring. Two of them belonged to the same outfit going together. The water was cold, and they were icing up pretty bad. One fellow said to the captain, "Don't you think we ought to stop and clean some of this ice off the boat? It's getting pretty top heavy." He says, "No, let the fellow that put it on take it off." Well, it was only about fifteen minutes, He did. Down the boat went. Sunk. And the fellows along with them come and took the fellows up.

This story has a religious moral; the captain seems to be blasphemous in his attitude and gets punished for it. This is similar to blasphemous captain stories told by commercial fishermen in the Gulf of Mexico (Mullen 1978b, 31–35), Maine (Beck 1957, 202) and elsewhere (Bassett 1885, 343–44). The story seems to be saying that fishermen have enough hardships in nature to face without also taking on supernatural forces.

Other stories about hazards are remembered because of the tragic results. George Wakefield recalled an incident from 1910.

One terrible accident occured off Cleveland Harbor. The "Silver Spray" I think the name was, the "Spray" I think the name was. They were fall fishing, winter fishing I guess you could call it, and they came, I think they lost pull, lost power, and they took to the board down at the pier down at Cleveland. They were stuck there. There was no way of getting in because there was ice all over the pier. They all froze to death.

The irony of being so close to the pier and still losing their lives is emphasized in the story. Perhaps it is significant that this was told by someone who is not a fisherman. Fishermen themselves did not tell of incidents in which lives were lost; their close-call stories stress survival, and they would not want to tell stories in which fishermen do not survive.

Bob Bodi and Martin Hosko told a survival experience they had together in extremely cold weather.

MH: We try to get the twine out just before the ice would come, you know. We wanted to fish as late as we could. Every once in awhile we got caught in the ice. That one winter he [Bodi] was talking about, oh that was late in December; I never abused a boat so much in my life. It was breaking eight inches of solid blue ice. We run around the ice, and bang, she would break over, lay over on her side, lay there a little while, and then start settling in the water. That would be completely out of water. We broke out the ice. It was eight below zero that morning. Remember, Bob? But we broke the ice to the lake, and we pulled the eighth net, and we had a hell of a bunch of fish. We had perch. Jerry was lifting ahead, and a little shallow ice was making while we was pulling them up, but we got our nets out. But it was eight below zero that morning he was talking.

BB: I'll never forget that day. I ain't got long to live according

to the doctor, but I'll never forget it. But Martin and the fellow
by the name of Dick Kientz, and Fred and Frank, we went out on
the pulling boat together, and it was so cold. Now Martin and I
and Dick, we was working. And I was sweating, and so was Dick.
Of course, when we get to the lead, Martin would run the boat
along the lead to make it come easier, you know. And Martin
hollered over to the lead boat, and said, "Come and get Frank off
of my boat." So they took him off. And first he tried to pick up a
fish, but his hands were so God durn cold, he couldn't. [The tape
was changed and the story continued later.] And it wasn't long till
he hollered to Jerry again, "Come and get Fritz," he said. So Jerry
come and got them, and Martin, Dick, and I finished up whatever
they was to pull, and came on in. But it was just so cold, that if
you would have kept them on the boat, God knows, they could
have stumbled, you know. You stumble on one of them boats.
MH: Everything was ice, you know.

Hosko and Bodi were caught in this situation because they tried to
go out too late in the fall. Once the cold weather sets in for good, Lake
Erie fishermen confine their activities to shore: making and mending
nets, repairing boats, and generally getting ready for the next fishing
season. A few men continue to fish commercially in the winter by going
out on the ice in cars and fishing through holes in the ice. This kind
of fishing had its own dangers, as Luke Gowitzka described.

And every once in a while the ice would break just like thunder.
Roars and water would come up maybe two foot in your hole.
And it scares you. Of course, we knew what was happening after
you fish awhile. We fished one day, and one of them big thunder
cracks come, and we got out of our shanty, and it was early.
There's a couple old guys whose crack broke right under their
shanty. Their shanty went down, but they got out. We went over
there to help get their shanty out. But three of them guys, I can
remember them going. One guy had an overcoat on. They had a
Coast Guard station at Marblehead. His old coattail was sticking
straight out. They was really flying, trying to go, scared to death.
Art and I went over, and these old guys, they got their crack
opened up. They jumped out of their shanty on ice, but the shanty
was sunk and started taking them. Anyhow, they just cut off a
piece of the ice that was left where they were on, and they chopped
a piece loose. Then they took their sled to use as a paddle and

pushed themselves back to the solid ice. I thought that was pretty smart of them.

One morning we come over, and there was just a spare tire sticking up. Guy's car was setting on its nose and just his spare tire was sticking out. The ice was pretty well messed up right around there. Took us a long time to cross over. We were a little scared. But you know, you go through that ice with your car and your doors aren't closed, no way you're gonna open that door up if you go down in the water with that pressure. So most of the time, I just stood on the running board of that old Ford, and just pushed the gas lever down and let her go.

Gowitzka's stories describe accidents that happened to other ice fishermen, but these incidents are reminders that the ice could give way under anyone at anytime.

Not all the dangers on the lake are from nature; the giant ore and gravel freighters that cut back and forth across Lake Erie are among the greatest hazards for small fishing boats. Chester Jackson and "Darby" Barrington both had close calls with freighters.

Mrs. Jackson: Tell him about your experience with the big steamboat.

Mr. J: I almost got sliced in two out there in the fog. You talk about your navigation. Two boats went out. I was working for Kishman at the time. The one boat was ahead, and he heard the steamboat. Of course, we don't have no exhaust on those boats, and they're noisy. I heard this swish, swish, swish. Turned around and right over my stern comes that big steamboat going by. Well, it was just seconds from me to slice me right in two. I never heard it. Of course, he heard me. He was probably blowing like hell, you know. But I got pretty shaky after that. I was awful leery of the fog after that. See, we'd go across the steamboat lines, steamship out of Lorain. There's a lot of them out there. You get to know the area after you fished, but that made me shaky, and after that I was really concerned with the fog.

DB: If it was foggy, you ain't gonna see nothing. [Laughs] That's miserable, oh that fog was something, you know, especially, you know, when you're getting out in a boat like that, and you know these damn big freighters are flying up and down the line there. God damn, boy, you know it is kinda scary. Cause, you know, you look, you happen to get one, near one of them in one of those little boats and look up at the bow of that thing, you know, why—

PM: Did you ever have any close calls with those?
DB: Yes, once goddamn it, with the "Big Chief" we were pulling, we was hooked on to a big long string of twine, way over near the, over near the Canadian, over near the line. We were pulling, it was little bit hazy, not too bad though, but then, we were pulling there, and Jesus, here we looked, I looked down the, out the side door, looked down there, and jeez I seen that big thing coming there, and I thought, "Holy Christ, I hope he can see us." And finally, all of a sudden, he must have spied us, you know, and he did sheer off away from us a little bit more.

The "freighter in the fog" stories symbolize the fisherman as the small individual who must contend not only with nature but also with huge impersonal vessels that are owned by large corporations. These big ships have the right of way on the lake, and the small fishing boats have to move aside or be run down. The small fishing boat is often owned by the man who is running it, and even if the captain is working for someone else, he is his own boss while on the water. Fishermen tell another kind of story in which they reject working for large companies where they lose their individuality (see chapter 5). Individuality is an important part of commercial fishermen's occupational identity, and the freighter stories offer another projection of this self-image.

Fishermen's stories reflect the many hazards they face in doing their job, but despite the risks involved, they continue in their chosen occupation. In fact, their narratives about almost sinking in storms, the extreme hardships of fishing in icy conditions, and close calls with freighters exhibit an occupational pride: they encounter these risks with courage, survive them, and go on fishing for a living. Several other kinds of stories Lake Erie commercial fishermen tell also indicate this positive occupational identity in even more complex ways.

5

Identity

The small group of commercial fishermen on western Lake Erie see themselves as hard-working, independent outdoorsmen, and their stories and comments embody this occupational identity. Because they are individualistic, their diverse personalities are revealed when they talk about occupational experiences. Their view of themselves as a group is not the same as the picture outsiders have of them: sport fishermen tend to see them as a threat to the fish population of the lake, wardens tend to see them as potential lawbreakers, and some of the townspeople along the coast view them as lazy alcoholics. All of these group and individual perspectives must be considered in order to understand the complex process of forming and maintaining occupational identity. We must look not only at the way fishermen see themselves but also at the way other people's views influence their self-image. This suggests that occupational identity comes both from within and from conflict with others (Dundes 1983; Spicer 1971). Although in-group and out-group dynamics are intimately bound together in the actual social context, we have divided the identity stories into two categories: one expresses identity both from within and through the influence of other groups (to be dealt with in this chapter), and the other type of story creates identity out of direct conflict with other groups (dealt with in the following chapter).

One of the negative stereotypes that outsiders have of commercial fishermen is that they are heavy drinkers, and this influences the way fishermen look at themselves. Several fishermen mentioned the stereotype even before we asked about it.

TL: What do fishermen do for recreation? I mean I'm sure they worked hard and worked long hours. Do fishermen spend time with one another or with one another's families when they are—?
Alva Snell: Well, the natural thought when you speak of a fisherman is he's going to spend his spare time in a bar.
TL: Is that true though?
AS: Well, I didn't drink, and I didn't smoke. But I spent a lot of my spare time just traveling. . . .
PM: So this stereotype of the fishermen drinking is just that, a stereotype? Some of them drink, but not all of them.
AS: But not all of them, no. I know another man here in town that I fished with. Took him out when he was young. I always took him on the boat when he was young, and I ended up fishing on a boat he was running down there fishing. He don't drink. Oh, he might take a drink, I don't mean that. But he's a hard worker, took care of his mother, and done all right. He owns about a dozen houses around town.

Snell emphasizes that he never drank and that the fishermen he admired did not drink to excess. He is very much aware of the negative stereotype, because he brought it up without us mentioning it, and he clearly contrasts the negative stereotype with the actuality as he perceives it. He even describes his nondrinking fellow worker as an all-around moral and upstanding citizen to make an even greater contrast with the stereotype. This tendency to put commercial fishermen in the best light fits with the way he told stories about Jib Snyder which de-emphasized his worst alcoholic traits (see chapter 3).

Snell did tell us about a fisherman who drank to the point that it interfered with his work.

Well, he was about the islands. Come this way and worked down here at Kishman's. Good fisherman, except that was one of his problems. He had to get through at a certain time to get up to the bar. That was the only bad thing I could say about him. He was a nice fellow and a good worker, but he just had to get up to the bar at a certain time. I know after I quit fishing here, I went down to Kishman's and worked for several years. I'd only been down there about a year. I was working with this Chester Jackson, and Ray [Full] called me in the office one day, and he says, "Could you tell me why it is Chester catches more fish than Stan [not his real name] does?" I said, "Maybe it's just right now we've got our nets in a little better place than he has. Maybe a few weeks from now, it will be the other way around." I wouldn't want to say anything about him, you know. But that was his problem. When the fish are around, you've got to get them cause two weeks from now, they're gonna be someplace else, and you have to put in a couple extra hours. Stan had the urge to get up to the bar at a certain time.

Here again Alva Snell only talks about a drunken fisherman in the context of a contrast with a nondrinking fisherman. Chester Jackson is the ideal hard worker, and although Stan works hard, his drinking interferes with his job performance.

Chester Jackson also talked about the drinking stereotype.

PM: Well, that's a stereotype some people have of the fishermen, the heavy drinkers.

CJ: Oh, yes.

PM: It's not just a stereotype? You mean some of them really were heavy drinkers?

CJ: Oh, yes.

PM: Was that ever a problem? You said he [another fisherman who was known as a drinker] was a hard worker. Anybody ever have any problems with him going out drunk fishing?

CJ: If he was drunk, by the time he got out there, he would sleep it off, and he always done his work. The captain couldn't carry a man if he didn't carry his own weight. The crew wouldn't put up with it. You were working commission. If you didn't do your own work, the crew wouldn't stand it. The captain wouldn't stand it either. Of course, I had a good reputation. Wasn't any drinking on my boat. I carried a bottle of whiskey always on the boat. I was the captain, and in the summertime, we would have a six-pack, one of these hook and liners [a small ice chest that sport fishermen carry beer in] when we come home. Always had some on the boat. Made a policy there was no drinking on the boat until on our way home. In the summertime, we would now and then, if we had beer on the boat, we would have a bottle of beer if we want it. But there was no drinking. I didn't have any drunks on my boat. I wouldn't stand for it. I don't drink myself to that extent.

A strong group identity will affect behavior; because fishermen shared the value of hard work and believed that drinking interfered with work, they would put pressure on the drinker to control his behavior. There was tolerance for drinking, but it ceased when drinking affected work.

Like Snell, Jackson mentioned Stan Oldquist [not his real name] as a heavy drinker.

CJ: Some of the captains would drink. I don't know if you've heard of Stan Oldquist, I don't know if his name come up or not. He's dead. Well, he was a good fisherman. He worked for Lay's for a long time, but he'd like to tip one or two. He was a good fisherman. . . . He worked for Lay Brothers a long time. He was a brute of a man, but the smoking and drinking got him. I don't know which caught him. He got cancer. He was a heavy smoker.

Jackson told another story about an excessive drinker who came to a bad end.

Years ago there was fellow here. I don't know if anybody told you or not, maybe Alva might have told you, but years ago, there used to be some of the gill-netters would come up from down the lake, and some of them would like to tip. Some of them would like their alcohol, you know. Tom Davis [not his real name] was, I ain't sure on that name, I think it's Tom Davis. But anyway, he was sleeping on the boat down there at Kishman's, and he was a good worker. Single, divorced or whatever or something, anyway, he was a man probably in his late forties, early fifties. Then when he got done with fishing, he would go up to the bar, and he wouldn't come back to the boat till he got stoned, you know. Drunker than a skunk. Only had one cop in town at the time, fellow by the name of Benson, but this time they turned the boat around on him. See, they always laid the boat the one way to the dock. This time for some reason or another, the boat got turned around.
Mrs. J: They probably did it for a trick.
CJ: No, they didn't. Maybe they were working on the boat or something, but afternoon, anyway they turned the boat around, so he knew how to get on his boat when he was drunk, but when the boat was turned around, he walked right in the river and stuck there. He died. Killed him.
Mrs J: I never knew that.
CJ: Yes, stuck in the mud, and hell, it was a couple days before he come up.

In both these stories, the heavy drinker died as a result of his drinking. Stan Oldquist died from excessive drinking and smoking, and Tom Davis died as a direct result of being drunk. Jackson and

Snell both make implicit moral points in their telling of these stories: the drinker is ultimately punished for his excesses.

Jackson told another story that reflects his awareness of the stereotyped view of commercial fishermen.

> I had a fellow by the name of Lawson [not his real name] worked for me years ago when I worked for Parson's, and a good worker. But his dad, he made his living marrying the old widows and killing them off. This is not conclusive, nothing to do with fishing, but anyway, Sammy [Lawson] quit. "What do you want to quit for?" "Oh," he says, "My dad says you don't want to be a drunken fisherman." See, that's the reputation. I said, "Well, you go home and tell your dad I'm no drunk, and I'll buy him out any day of the week." You know, he was marrying these old women, they'd die, and then he'd get the money. That's how he made his living. Now, Alva don't drink. Alva Snell don't drink. I'll have a highball, I'll have a bottle of beer, you know. It's no secret, but I never drank on the job. Couldn't see it.

Jackson contrasts the stereotype with his and Snell's actual behavior and points out the hypocrisy of the outsider who criticizes fishermen for drinking when the outsider is guilty of a graver immorality.

Some fishermen seem to accept the stereotype of the drunken fisherman: Lewis Keller stated, "All the fishermen drank. I don't give a damn who it was. Every Saturday morning we'd all end up in one big bar, and we'd drink beer till hell wouldn't have it." Like Snell and Jackson's testimony, his description suggests drinking as a leisure not a work activity, and his wife recalled the same thing.

> **PM:** So, you worked hard, but what did you do for recreation or a good time?
> **LK:** Drink. I used to drink plenty when I was younger.
> **PM:** And that's what most of the fishermen did?
> **LK:** Most of them. Oh, we would have parties and stuff like that, too.
> **Mrs. K:** I heard that one. Stop at a bar. They'd all meet in there and talk about the day's work. In them days, you bought a bottle of beer for a dime, glass of beer a nickel a mug. They'd gather in there and talk and laugh about the different things that happened. They worked on different boats.

Lewis Keller's statement and his wife's description indicate that drinking was a widespread leisure activity that probably reinforced the popular view of commercial fishermen as alcoholics. In the face of this, Keller's comment projects pride in their drinking; unlike Jackson and Snell, he does not mind reinforcing the stereotype. He sees drinking as part of the fisherman's occupational identity, a masculine declaration of independence.

There were distinct types of commercial fishing, and one group held stereotypes about the other, as "Darby" Barrington revealed.

PM: Were fishermen, did fishermen have the reputation of being drinkers?
DB: Well, yeah, two-thirds of them did; all that I knew did. Gillnetters, they were, they were a bunch of dudes; they were doozies too, gill-netters.

Here again, though, the extent of drinking is qualified; at least some fishermen did not drink.

A related stereotype of fishermen held by many outsiders is that they are always filthy, even when not working. The character anecdotes related in chapter 3 often turn upon this trait. Bob Bodi and Martin Hosko talked about this and connected it to drinking.

BB: You would buy a suit of overalls, jacket and overalls, you know. And the fishermen at that time, I can remember when I was a kid, they'd come up there to the saloon and the biggest part of the fishermen, outside of the fellows that run the rig, it was kind of a boozer's life. They would buy, like I say, a suit of overalls, and then they would wear them till they would stand up by theirselves.
MH: Not all of us, Bob. Nearly every week you had a clean one and so did I, but a lot of them would wear them, by God, till they had so much tar you could stand them up almost, without wind would stand up. But not my crew. I wouldn't let anybody go that long. "Hey, how about some clean clothes or something," I would tell them.
PM: There were some guys in other crews though that would?
MH: Some of them were awful filthy, dirty, you know. It was a dirty work, and a lot of them didn't keep themselves clean.

Once the trait of dirtiness is mentioned, Hosko is quick to disassociate both men from it.

Later in the same conversation Bodi talked about how clean they kept the boat. "And Martin would meet me down to the dock, and help unload and everything, and you could drop a sandwich in the bilge of that boat, and you could pick it up and eat it. It was that clean." However, given the nature of the work, it was almost impossible to stay clean, and anyone who did was viewed negatively.

MH: John Dawson [not his real name], he'd have a clean shirt in the morning, white cuffs rolled up, and by noon, he'd go to dinner, and come back with another clean shirt. He wouldn't pick up a piece of rope or he wouldn't pick up a box or nothing. Just real refined kind. And he was being took blind, stole blind. I mean I could see it because maybe I was more interested in it than any of my men because I was owner, but you see some of those things going on, and if some of them don't make money, it ain't hard to figure out why.

Because fishermen have a long off-season during which they do not appear to be working, some townspeople view them as lazy. The fishermen themselves emphasize what hard workers they are in their stories about the old days (see chapter 2) and in statements about their personal values. Two fishermen in particular, Chester Jackson and Alva Snell, stressed their individual belief in the work ethic. Jackson was the more emphatic.

In fact, I had the reputation that a lot of people wouldn't work under me because they called me "Slavedriver" Jackson. You can put that in the article. I don't mind it. I am a slave driver. I'm still a driver. But I worked right with my men. I always wanted to be top-notch. To be top-notch, you had to give the extra effort, put in the extra hours.

Jackson is clearly proud of his "slavedriver" reputation because it meant he was a big producer. He was a success at his job because he worked his men hard, but like the image of John Lay, his self-image shows him working just as hard as his men. There is an egalitarian value along with the work ethic.

Jackson and Snell both mentioned competition as part of their work ethic. Jackson first described the hard work in detail and then suggested why he worked so hard.

It was a hard, heavy job. I didn't realize at the time I come off the farm. I told Mrs. Jackson afterwards. I says, "I ought to be crazy to fish along the lake." Really a hard—your face would burn, your skin would crack. I got a skin cancer. Alva's got several cancers from it. And the tar. But I enjoyed every minute of it. I would have probably done the same thing. It's a challenge out there. You didn't know what you was going to get till you got out there. They work hard all their life. Of course, I always wanted to be top dog. Alva in town here, he was the same way. He run his own rig for a long time. His boys went into industry. Sort of a challenge to see who had the best lift that day.

In a separate interview, Alva Snell expressed many of the same beliefs and associated them with Jackson.

PM: What makes a good fisherman?
AS: Well, Chester Jackson and I were both saying the same thing: you gotta be hungry. He was and I was, see. And we talked about it a lot of times. Says you gotta be hungry, gotta want to make some money. Figure that's a way of doing it; well, you put in a few more hours and work a little harder. Now, Chester, he started out, he was as poor as they could be. Didn't have anything, but he was a hard worker, and he worked hard and got to be a good fisherman. Saved his money, and—[the tape ran out; after a new one was started, Snell continued].

That's right. You had to produce more than the other fellow. Then you was the one that was making the money. I know when I went to Lorain to fish after I got off the boat you took the picture of, you know, they had four trap-net boats there at that time. And I didn't have unemployment those days, and for trap-netters, you worked in the wintertime. They fixed up their nets for spring, you know, and I needed the work. I couldn't be laid off all winter, so I went trap netting. Well, I only trap netted there not over a couple years, and I was on the outfit, and he came to me one winter when we got through, and he says, "You're to run a boat in the spring." Well, land, I was only a young fella, and I said, "I don't think that's gonna work. You got men that's been here for years. What are they gonna think, seeing a young fella like me running the boat?" He says, "That's the trouble with them." He says, "They don't know any more now than they did twenty years ago. I want you to run the boat." "Well, okay." Well, right away I was high boat. I mean I caught more fish than the rest of them. Every Saturday night, payday, you know, they come to me. "Well, you want to work tomorrow?" Cause everything that needs to be done, they'd ask me. And if I says yes, we should do so and so. "Okay, take the whole day, and we'll work tomorrow." Well, I wanted to work. I was hungry. I needed the money. And it used to kind of get some of the other fellas. They would say, "My God, his outfit and he asked him," young fella like me, "if we ought to work tomorrow." But I was hungry. I was like Jackson, you know. He wanted to work, so that's the way it is.

All of the fishermen talked about how hard the work was, but Snell and Jackson had personal identities more strongly based on the work ethic. In America, the work ethic is related to achievement orientation and competition (Atkinson 1958; McClelland 1961), and in this way Alva Snell's narrative is an American success story. He and Jackson started out poor, but through hard work and competition achieved success in their chosen occupation.

Other kinds of personal identity occur within the stories about the occupational group. This indicates the multiple nature of identity within one group; a fisherman defines himself by his occupation but also through other values and associations (Dundes 1983; Zavalloni 1983). For instance, Martin Hosko revealed his personal identity as an owner when he talked about the way he ran his fish company.

I tell you it's wonderful. Some employers don't pay no attention to their help. I did. I knew every one personally. I knew their families. I knew their kids. I had one big clown, weighed about two hundred and fifty pounds, liked to clown, always clowning. "Well, what do you want me to do, boss?" "Well," I say, "Chuck, I'll tell you what. I want you in charge, I want every speck of tar off these trucks, and I want them simonized. I want underneath greased, cleaned out of old grease, clean them out." He had a nice place to work, a nice warm place, jack them up, and clean up all the dirt underneath them, spray them with the paint or undercoating, rustproof them, change oil, grease the trucks up, and everything you know. He'd say to me, "Boss, I just changed oil in that truck." I'd say, "Change it again." In fact, used to buy oil for sixty-eight cents a gallon, detergent oil, good detergent oil. "Grease them, wash them, do what I tell you to do." "Martin, I'll be all winter." "Don't you want to work all winter?" He had another clown working with him, you know. He wasn't too good in the twine, but he was good helping him out. When my trucks went out on the road, they look like a brand new truck if they was ten years old.

Hosko sees himself as a working fisherman and also as an owner, an identity he does not share with most of the fishermen we interviewed. He projects an image as owner that is close to that of John Lay in the stories told about him: he expects his men to work hard, but he is a kind and generous boss in return.

Those fishermen whose fathers, grandfathers, or sons were or are in fishing stressed family heritage as part of their occupational identity. Lewis Keller's father was a fisherman who got Keller into the business at an early age, thus helping to establish his identity. Alva Snell talked about his father, grandfather, and great-grandfather being fishermen (see chapter 2), and he recalled how this influenced his decision to become a fisherman.

> When I started out, the first job I had on the lake, I went out on the boat he [his father] was running. Of course, I had an older brother who was a fisherman all his life, too. And, oh yes, all kinds of stories if they would come to me. I used to know a man that married one of my granddaughters here just a couple weeks ago. And he says, "Did you really want to be a fisherman?" I said, "Yes, I couldn't hardly wait till I got big enough to go out on them boats." I seen them all and thought that was wonderful to get on them boats, you know. That's what I wanted to do.

The family connection goes in both generational directions: fishermen whose sons become fishermen also emphasize the unity of family and occupational identity. Luke Gowitzka mentioned that his son had become a commercial fisherman, and Paul Leidorf and Joe Herr see themselves in the middle of a father-to-son lineage.

> **PL:** I was on a boat before I even walked. I started working on a boat when I was about four years old. Not working, but at least the old man was working and getting me out of the way.
> **JH:** Well, look at my kids too.
> **PL:** Yes, Joe's boys are the same. Raised on these [boats].

Herr, Leidorf, Keller, and Snell are good examples of the process of internalization (Vogt 1955): their identities as fishermen began to be formed in childhood because of family tradition. Going out on boats at an early age helps to internalize this identity, and the influence of a father is even stronger.

When a man grows up in a fishing family, the occupation of fishing "gets in his blood," as the fishermen we talked to often said. In fact, this phrase was repeated more often than any other when fishermen tried to explain their love of fishing.

PM: Well, there must be something you guys like about it to put up with all these headaches all these years.
Joe Herr: Hey, we're free men. Hell, we're free men.
Paul Leidorf: Once it gets in your blood, you'll probably. You say you was coming from the [Gulf] Coast, and you probably was in with the shrimp industry there. Once you get on a boat, there is something about a boat you can't describe. It gets in your blood, and once it's in your blood, and you stay at it.

Larry Davis said, "When you get enough of that fish slime in your blood stream, you never get it out." Even when the expression "in your blood" did not occur in their explanations, fishermen expressed a sense of deep attachment to commercial fishing.

"Darby" Barrington: But you know, it was something that was fascinating, when you got into it, you, you, it just seemed you couldn't get away from it. Got out on the water, got working on the water, you know, and everything, it was just fascinating there. I was there for about forty years.

Alva Snell expressed his love of fishing in a different way.

TL: Everyone says it's hard work, but everyone says they wouldn't have it any other way. Why do you think that is? Why do people like it?
AS: Well, I don't know. One of them things. I was just reading an article in paper, magazine tells what percentage of people don't like their jobs. A big percentage of them didn't like their jobs. They had to work out somewhere, and they wanted to get away, retire. I never felt that way. Of course, on the other hand, I didn't have too much as a kid. I was brought up poor. My father was a fisherman, and he drank, you know, like most fishermen, so we didn't have too much. If I wanted anything, I had to get up and get it. A fellow older than I was I knew real well used to have a saying. He says, "A poor man should get his pleasure from his work." You know, that's true. If you like your job, like me, I don't play golf, I don't play bingo, nor anything. I do like to travel.

Fishermen had a hard time articulating their love of their work; Barrington resorts to repeating the word "fascinating," Snell uses a proverbial saying, and others fall back on the expression "it gets in your blood." Snell explains why occupation is so important with the idea that a working man should get pleasure from his work because most of his life is spent at it, and he does not have much time for leisure activities. This is an idea that could be applied to many working-class occupations besides fishing.

Nearly every fisherman we interviewed illustrated his attachment to his occupation with a particular story based on his own personal experience. These stories differed in detail, of course, but the underlying pattern was the same. Even the way the telling of the story came about in the interview followed a recurring pattern. After a fisherman described all of the hardships and difficulties of commercial fishing, we would ask him why he continued to fish, and he would respond with his personal version of this narrative. Paul Leidorf told a brief story that encapsulates the pattern.

> I've had good jobs, and I've had enough education that I could [make a] go in [other jobs]. I've been in like . . . bearings and working on transmissions. I hated that so bad. I knew how many steps it took to get there, and it didn't take as many steps to get out, cause they were a little bit longer. There's just something about it. I basically spent my life, you might say, on the lake.

The pattern of quitting fishing, working in a factory or some other land-based job, being dissatisfied with that, and returning to the lake illustrates the basic idea: fishing has a way of getting in your blood. Trying other kinds of work is never successful because the love of fishing is so ingrained that it is inevitable that the fisherman will return to the water.

Alva Snell's experience working in a factory made such an impression on him that he mentioned it twice in one interview. The two versions are almost identical so that only one is cited.

> I started out gill netting, and years ago there was no one informed of anything like there is today. I got married and had children, and no work in the wintertime. So you would be on a gill net, and by the time you rigged up, it's spring, and so it wasn't always easy to find a job. I worked the steel plant one winter till almost spring. I couldn't stand it any longer. I didn't like [being] cooped up inside, so I quit, and then I went trap netting because they had work in the wintertime mending nets.

Chester Jackson also emphasized the contrast between indoor and outdoor work. "I went over to Elyria and worked a few weeks in a factory, but that ain't for me. I like the outdoors." Jackson's and Snell's preferences for outdoor work relate to their hazard stories, which emphasize the fisherman's work context in nature, but even more important in the "in your blood" stories is the negative attitude toward factory work in contrast to working on the lake.

There were other significant variations on the alternative work place. Bob Bodi's version of the story, for instance, contrasts fishing with another outdoor occupation, railroading, but he still chose fishing despite higher wages on the railroad. Martin Hosko worked longer at a factory job and had more incentives to stay, but he also eventually returned to fishing.

So I worked at Bissell's there. And when I worked there all winter, now we got five dollars a day, fifty cents an hour, ten hours we worked. I worked there all winter, and I got so I could run the lathe, I could run any drill presses and punch press or whatever was to run, and anyway, Old Man Bissell, he thought I was something. Now, spring come, and I'm thinking, my father-in-law was foreman, and Beddington was superintendent. They used to go eat together, and naturally I would go with them. Everybody pay for their dinner. So I'd be walking the spring of the year, when it was time to go in the lake, we'd be walking to dinner, and I would be thinking to myself how I'd love to be out on the lake. It would be a nice day, a nice breeze blowing. I'd love to be out on the lake now.

So I says to my father-in-law, I says, "Pappy," I says, "You know, I don't think I can stay here this summer. I think I'm going to quit." "Oh, don't do that. Bissell thinks the world and all. Oh, he's talking about giving you a raise to seventy-five cents an hour." And working for a dollar a day and my board, and going to give me seventy-five cents an hour, ten hours at seven fifty for ten hours work. I thought, I got to thinking about it, and when I got thinking about being out in the lake, I quit anyway. I had that in my blood. I wanted to be out there on the water. Like Bob said, it was something different everyday. Didn't make no difference. It might have been a bad day today and tomorrow, but tomorrow it might have been a real nice day, and you forgot all what happened. But I quit seven dollars and fifty cents a day job for a dollar a day and my board.

Every fisherman we interviewed either told an "in your blood" story or expressed the same attitudes in more general statements. For instance, Luke Gowitzka did not tell a self-contained narrative, but in talking about his work experiences on land he made his preference for fishing clear. Lewis Keller, on the other hand, told a fully developed narrative about his factory experience. He emphasized his independence, a value espoused by most fishermen.

PM: How did she [his wife] feel about your fishing? Did she prefer for you to fish or to work some other jobs?
LK: Oh, hell, she didn't have nothing to say. Hell, you did what you wanted to. I fished all my life, and that's the way I'm going to be. There was nobody. I was kind of independent, you know. One year, during the war, everybody was making that big money. I was working for Brown's at that time or where, I don't remember now. It was during the war anyway. I think I was working for Brown, and I got a job at the Plumbrook Ordnance out there. I was in the acid gang. We was making pretty good money, see? I forget now what the hell it was, but anyway, I was up there supposed to be next to be a pumper, and the pumper he made more money than the other guys did, see. Well, Jesus Christ, it come time for me to get promoted, I didn't get promoted. Some guys come up from down in Tennessee or from the South. That's where half of them were from anyway. They catered to those guys, so they got the job pumping. I had to work under them then. Yet, I was there longer than they were. So, I got mad, you know, and the hell with this job. So, I went over to the office, and I told them I was quitting. "You can't quit." "What do you mean, I can't quit?" "You gotta stay on this job as long as the war is going on." I said, "Listen, I was never on a job in my life that I couldn't quit."

Boy, I knew I was going to go back fishing at the time. But they sent me up to the office. Well, then they'd go in one office, and they'd send me to another office. And that guy would send me to another one, see, and it was like that all day long. So the next day I went out there again to get my termination papers and my pay. "You can't quit." "I never had a job in my life I couldn't quit." So I went after one guy, and he sent me to another guy. Same ones they sent me to the day before. Well, I found out this one guy, the first guy, was the guy that wouldn't do me any good, so went back up to his office. I said, "Listen now, I've done all the God damn fooling around and running around I'm gonna do." I said, "I want out of here, and I want out of here now." "Where you gonna work?" I said, "On the lakes." And that's all I said, and by golly, he gave me my pay. I went back fishing. I never cared for that kind of work in the first place. It's all right in the wintertime, but, boy, in the summertime, that's for the birds.

This story gives the most detailed contrast between factory work and fishing. The factory is described as a labyrinth of bureaucratic red tape in which the individual is completely lost. No one cared that Keller had been unjustly passed over for promotion, and when he tried to quit, the impersonality of the place became even more apparent as he was sent from one office to another. His greatest anger comes when he is told that he cannot quit; this is an affront to his sense of freedom and individuality, and he becomes the hero of his own story because he stands up for his rights. Throughout the description of the factory bureaucracy, there is an implied contrast to working on the lake where a man is free from this kind of control. Keller's narrative is the commercial fishermen's version of the "take this job and shove it" story popularized in the country song by Johnny Paycheck, an American workingman's statement of defiance against the system that exploits him.

Lewis Keller's wife told a story about him that is a variation on the usual pattern but still expresses the idea of fishing getting "in your blood."

Well, when he was telling when he left Lay Brothers and went over to Lakeside, the reason he had to leave Lay Brothers was because he had arthritis or rheumatism in your legs, and he had to go to the doctor with it, and the doctor told him, "Boy, you're going to have to get away from that water. That's what's causing it. Try to get a job away from the water." And so he told Lay Brothers. Then he went to look for a job. He left one morning, and came back that afternoon and said, "Well, I got a job. We're going to have to move." He said, "The boss is renting us a house over in Erie Beach." I said, "What kind of a job is it?" He said, "Running party boats." I said, "Lewie, that's on the water. You're supposed to get away from the water." He said, "I can't get away from the water." He said, "This way I won't be on it for much," getting wet like he did fishing. He couldn't give up that fishing.

Currently active commercial fishermen share the same strong occupational identity that the old-timers such as Lewis Keller have, but they are very pessimistic about their chances of survival. Joe Herr and Paul Liedorf were talking about how long it takes to train a man before he can go out on his own.

JH: Takes five years to get a man broke in right, before he can handle the twine, bend it off, and that kind of stuff. Five years experience. And a man with five years experience ain't going to stick around with us guys.
PM: Oh, you mean they'll go and get a boat of their own?
JH: They can't. . . . If I go in the grave, my license goes with it. I can't even give it to my kids.
PL: That's another thing to screw us up. There is no way we can sell this stuff to go back into commercial industry. If we die, the license is shot. We don't take our license out in two years, it's shot, gone. Put in escrow, and whether you fish it or not, and then if you don't fish it at the end of the first year, the second year you fish it, they double the royalty on it. It's asinine, what's going on really.
JH: It's frozen.
PL: Like politics, it has gotten way out of hand.
JH: There's twenty licenses left, but there's already Turinsky's license in the box with him.
PL: When Turinsky died, [someone else] tried to buy the license. Had everything all set up, paid them for it. And our twine rotted while they were in court.
JH: And they never got the license. It went into the grave with him. When Tony Turinsky died, they put the license in the box, right in the grave. Dead. Gone.

Identity is dynamic; it changes through time because of social change (Goodenough 1963). Even though there has been a persistence of occupational identity from Lewis Keller's, Bob Bodi's, and Alva Snell's time to the present, the statements by younger men such as Joe Herr and Paul Leidorf indicate that fishermen's identity has changed in the eighties. The forces that they perceive as working against them have worn them down. They may survive personally in the occupation, but they do not see much chance for the occupation surviving on Lake Erie after they are gone.

It is clear from these stories that commercial fishermen on western Lake Erie share a strong occupational identity. The fact that they all tell variations on what is essentially the same story is an indication of group values including independence, hard work, and a love for the outdoors. Even with all of these shared values, though, fishermen are also individuals, and personal traits are reflected in their narratives.

Despite, or perhaps because of, all of the hardships associated with fishing as an occupation, they have an almost mystical attachment to it. Their dedication to fishing is strengthened by the human forces that they see working against them, as exemplified in their conflicts with sport fishermen, wardens, and other outsiders.

6

〰〰〰〰〰

Conflict

Lake Erie commercial fishermen perceive a complex array of forces working against them: government regulations and the game wardens who enforce them, sport fishermen and tackle manufacturers who cater to the sport, and Canadian fishermen who have more lenient regulations. Each of these groups is viewed negatively in the stories fishermen tell about their contacts with them. At the same time that these stories project negative images of outsiders, they reinforce by contrast the positive image fishermen have of themselves. This oppositional identity (Dundes 1983; Spicer 1971) is an important factor in understanding how fishermen shape and project identity through personal experience narratives.

Government agencies, game wardens, sport fishermen, and tackle manufacturers blame the decline of the fish population in Lake Erie at least partially on commercial fishing, but the fishermen themselves see pollution as the main cause of poor fishing. Lewis Keller was emphatic in blaming the decline on pollution.

> In fact, there'd be a lot of fish yet today, but they all claim that the commercial fisherman caught all the pickerel, and they caught all the blue pike, and all the saugers, and the whitefish, and everything else. Well, I don't believe that. I can't and never will because your pollution is what caused most of your trouble today.

Martin Hosko also blamed pollution for the decline of fishing in Lake Erie; he outlined the history of pollution in the lake.

MH: Yes, at one time we would get a ton of walleyes in one net between Big Sister and Little Sister [Islands]. Do you know where that is? Well, we used to have about eighty nets in the spring of the year. And, it got so, after about ten years fishing, that water started turning brown something like this table. It got browner every year. It kept getting worse and worse. And it was right there right between the islands, between Monroe, Stony Point, Little Sister, West Sister, and the islands down like that. We had to quit fishing there. Only place you could fish was on the beach where they could get air. See, that was rotten water out there. We had to quit fishing there. . . . Now, at the time, they used to have a huge, about a twenty-four foot pipe going out. Used to be red water going into the Maumee River. And even carp wouldn't live in that water. Used to wash steel and whatever they used, and the water must have had a lot of acid in it. It would kill carp right there. So the pickerel couldn't go up the river and spawn. . . . But the commercial fishermen got blamed for it. We was the goats. Still are. I feel sorry for commercial fishermen. I made a good living, and commercial fishing was wonderful to me. The longer I fished, the better it was.

TL: How many fishermen were there in 1940 on the western part of the lake?

MH: Well in 1940 there was eight thousand five hundred trap nets fishing in Ohio, eight thousand five hundred. The state has a record of that. And I think we're down to three hundred nets, and they want to eliminate that.

Alva Snell and Chester Jackson agree with the assessments of Hosko and Keller.

AS: And, of course, there have been a lot of theories as to what the reason, but the hook and line fishermen will tell you that commercial fishermen fished them out, of course. But it was DDT. . . . That's all there was to it; that ended the blue pike. And the same way with other fish. They say, "Well, what happened to the sturgeon? Well, what happened to the whitefish?" Same thing happened. Civilization, the change, the water quality changed, and they just couldn't survive. That's the way I look at it.

CJ: There's just a pittance out there what it used to be. Gosh almighty. That's why I quit fishing. It wasn't because I was old though I was sixty-two. I fished forty-one years. But I've worked my butt off. We set our nets like we did for years, and we'd always get lots of production. The last couple years I fished, I just got disgusted. It's like butting your head up against a wall and getting no return. . . . Now they blame the commercial fishermen. The last hatch of blue pike that hatched out here was in about '52 or '53. But this was caused from the DDT they used in World War II. The farmers used it for weed control. It took that many years for it to get into the water stream.

The fishermen are in complete agreement that pollution is the main cause of the decline of fish in the lake, and it is a problem that is out of their control. They all speak about the unfairness of blaming them for the demise of fish when the evidence clearly points to pollution. Their comments about pollution function to take the blame off of them and project an image of fishermen as innocent bystanders in the ruination of the lake.

Because commercial fishermen are seen as contributors to the fish decline, laws have been passed to restrict the size and species they may catch, and state game wardens are assigned to enforce these laws. Every fisherman has had numerous contacts with game wardens, and they tell stories based on their ongoing conflicts. One of these stories was passed down from one generation to another.

Alva Snell: Yes, there's always been some law as far as I can remember. Then I've heard stories cause I said my father and grandfather and great-grandfather were fishermen. They tell a story about my grandfather who was running a gill-net boat down there at Fairport Harbor, and the game warden was on the boat. They were into the dock, you know, working. Been out fishing. The game warden was on the dock giving them a hard time. What it was about I don't know. All I know is the story they tell, and finally one of the fellows throwed the lines off the stern of the boat, and somebody else on the front of the boat pushed the boat out, and they started down the river. The warden says, "Where we going?" My grandfather said, "We're going out in the lake and drown you." You see, there was laws back, that was a long time ago.

Snell's grandfather's comic threat against the warden probably expresses a repressed desire of many present-day fishermen. They feel hostility toward some game wardens, but of course they cannot openly express it. The stories give an acceptable outlet for venting these hostilities.

Their main complaint is with what they perceive as the unfairness and uneven enforcement of the laws. Snell tells a story that illustrates this complaint.

PM: Did the boat you were on ever have any conflicts with game wardens?
AS: Oh, yes, I got arrested many times. A place down here, that fish market, a fellow come along and wanted to know if he could go out on the lake with us. I said, "Sure." After we got out there, he wanted to help, you know. He was real interested and wanted to help, and he was sorting fish. You know, you get small fish in the dip nets. You know, you see how they done it up there. You got to get the big ones out and throw the little ones overboard. Well, he wanted to help, and he was sorting fish. We was clear out by the line by the Canadian border a ways away. And we came in and went to unload our fish, and there was the game warden on the dock. He looked the fish over and had too many small ones. You're allowed a percentage for mistake, but we had too many, and I had never had any trouble before, but I figured that fellow that was sorting, he hated to throw them away. We're used to throwing them away, but he throwed too many in, and they took my whole catch. It was Thursday, and I wanted to fish for fish market for Friday. They took the whole catch, and I got arrested, of course. Same time I went over to one of the other fish markets. The fellow that was buying it was from Canada. Hell, he had smaller fish than I did. They let him get away with it. I couldn't.

The innocent fisherman who is only trying to be a nice guy gets arrested because of the mistake of another, but even more frustrating for Snell is the fact that the laws protect another person who is selling even smaller fish. Frustration is a recurring theme in fishermen's warden stories.

Snell also talked about another situation that most fishermen think is unfair: the border between the United States and Canada establishes an arbitrary boundary for regulations even though the fishing is all done in the same body of water.

Years ago, you know, if you didn't have good fishing on this side, you went over to the Canada side and tried it. They had a couple Canadian boats over the years, the "Vigilante" was one of them, and I forget the name of the other one. Now, the fish would run down the line. They started up the other end of the lake, and run down what they supposed was half way across the lake, you know, or wherever the boundary was, and then if they see any boats, why, they would chase after them. But, Lord, they had big smokestack on them, steamboat you know. You could see them for ten miles. No trouble to get away from them most of the time. Most of the time you wouldn't get caught. When I was young, the fishing was good here on this side. You didn't have to go over, but if you thought it was better over there, well, let's go over and try it over there. So you'd go. And sometimes you would go over, well, just a little while before dark, you know, and set your nets, and lay there, and in the morning back you'd come. Wanted to find out if the fish was there.

Snell said that Canadian fishermen fish on the American side and use tricks to hide their presence such as marking their nets with Christmas trees instead of the usual flags. Fishermen on both sides tend to view the boundary as an artificial restriction of their freedom to pursue their occupation where they see fit.

According to Joe Herr, the situation has gotten even worse because fishermen on the United States side cannot bring in walleye and the Canadians can.

And they tell us that there is a hell of a demand for pickerel [walleye] around here because Jim [Van Hoose] in the [Port Clinton] fish house, in pickerel season in Canada, he goes three times a week to get a truckload of pickerel. Three truckloads a week so he can supply the restaurants and anybody, people that come in and want to buy them. We catch them out there by the [island]. We got to throw them back over the side, and the guy that's just over the line, he catches them, brings them into Canada, loads them on his truck, he pulls right in here. I come in and throw two thousand pounds over the side in a day. I come in here and tie the boat up, and I'm unloading twenty boxes of fish, and the truck backs in, and I'm sure as I'm sitting here some of the fish that come off that truck in Canada, I already threw over the side because I can see the damn boats out there, you know, where I'm fishing. Then they come right in here, and them Canadians are getting, what, a buck or a buck and a quarter a pound for them. And I throw them over the side so they can bring them in right back here, and they go to any restaurant you go to around here has got pickerel, any one. All comes from Canada, the other side of the pond. Our neighbors, but we gotta throw them all back.

Again the note of frustration over the perceived unfairness of the

laws comes into a fisherman's commentary. It is especially irritating to
Ohio fishermen that the same fish they have to throw back can be
caught by Canadian fishermen and sold in Ohio restaurants only a
block from where they tie up their boats.

Chester Jackson has had some encounters with wardens, and he also
thinks enforcement has become more strict over the years.

PM: Did you ever have any run-ins with them?
CJ: Oh, off and on. I mean if a man told you he didn't have a
run-in once in awhile. They would always measure your fish. I
think maybe they might have been a little more lenient in the
thirties. They'd warn you maybe once or twice a little bit more
than they would in the fifties and sixties and seventies. Then, of
course, as the sports writers and the hook-and-line fishermen got
predominantly strong, well, they'd get I'd say a little bit more, well
say cocky, but that may not be the word, more strict in their
reading the letter of the law. . . . When you handle this many fish,
it's easy to go both ways. You try not to. Nobody wants to be fined.
They can close you up and take your license away. I never was
afraid of them. I always tried to stay within the law, but I'm sure
I violated a lot of times, like a man driving a car would go through
a stop light. I think anyone tells you different, they are not telling
the truth.

Jackson's comment about sports writers and hook-and-line fishermen is typical of the comments of most commercial fishermen. They
see various forces in league against them. They feel that sport fishermen have influenced legislation for strict regulation, but that then the
laws are not applied equally to sport and commercial fishing.

Paul Leidorf talked about the unfairness of the laws.

PL: They've got more game wardens than there is fishermen.
PM: What's the story with the sport fishermen?
PL: They check them for their license, occasionally they check
them for their license. They are getting maybe one out of a half
percent that they check. They got a guy that goes down to the
different marinas and fish companies that's cleaning fish. They
get seasick out on the lake, so they can't check the people out
there, so he checks them in there, and then they come along and
punch their calculator.

Leidorf's comic remark about game wardens getting seasick barely
conceals a more serious contempt for many of them. Mentioning the

calculator also makes the warden out to be a desk-bound bureaucrat, implicitly contrasted with the freedom-loving outdoors fisherman.

Lewis Keller is even more direct in his criticism of the competence of game wardens.

Yes, that's when I was fishing for Bickley down there. One of the old-time game wardens come in there with two young fellows one day. They had just come out of college. Didn't even know what the hell a fish looked like. Came in there, and he was going through all the boxes and showing them what a blue pike looked like, and a sauger, a sheepshead, perch. "Now put it down in your mind now what they are." That's what they learned what a fish was. They maybe never seen a fish before like that. But that's the way they learned. They would go in there to be a conservationist for trees and wildlife and stuff like that. They don't go there to— now I guess they do. I don't know. I imagine they do. They study up on fishing.

Both Keller and Leidorf view wardens as school-educated, which means they do not know as much about fish and the lake as commercial fishermen who have been educated through experience.

Because fishermen think wardens are incompetent and the laws unfair, incidents in which wardens were fooled or a case was won against them in court become the subject of personal stories. Keller told about breaking the law and almost getting caught.

PM: You told me one time you were, you almost had a run-in with the game warden.

LK: When the guy was waving us down? Well, they used to come down there during the week, and we never used to, oh, we did a little outlawing, I'll say that, but who in the hell didn't in those days; they all did the same thing. But, these guys, they was just bound and determined they was laying for us that day. Just luck, there was a couple guys down there, you know, coming in that knew us, that hailed us down, so we went back out and unloaded. So when we come in, we didn't have nothing.

PM: How did they warn you? How did they get word to you?

LK: When they was waving us down like that up there [pointing to his chest where the wardens wear their badges], we knew there was something wrong at the dock. That's how they could tell, when they was waving you down like that, you know, as much as to say go back out cause you knew there was something wrong on that dock in there.

PM: How did you get rid of the fish?
LK: Just threw them overboard. Sea gulls had a picnic. I'll never forget that day. The poor guy that was with us that day, he cried.

Not all the fishermen admit intentionally breaking the law, but Lewis Keller and several others do not mind projecting an implicit outlaw image of fishermen in the stories they tell. This places these occupational narratives in the tradition of American outlaw heroes such as Jesse James, Sam Bass, and "Pretty Boy" Floyd (Dorson 1959, 236–43), and as in those legends the outlaw is seen as justified in his actions because of unjust laws. There is a sense here of a folk justice, a higher moral than the legislated laws (Mullen 1978a).

Because commercial fishermen see themselves as beleaguered by unreasonable laws and attacked by groups that are trying to put them out of business, some fishermen have responded with an explicit outlaw image of themselves reminiscent of Clifford Baker's attitude toward his liquor-running exploits (see chapter 3).

Frank Jones [not his real name]:   For what amount of us is here, and what amount is there, they are checking us ninety percent compared to maybe one tenth of what they are checking on them [sport fishermen].
Sam Barnes [not his real name]:   They're laying them to us.
FJ: They know we're in the under position, and ain't gonna take the chance. [But] you know, if you're hurting, and before you let all this equipment go, you're gonna outlaw. I mean very few times I have, but I'll tell you at times I have because it was either that or lose the outfit. And when you start losing the outfit, you're losing your family with it. You put everything right down to the nitty-gritty, and penny to penny, if they throw you in jail, they gotta feed your family. And that's the way you look at it.
SB: Us guys got pretty good families cause they stick with us. They got to be pretty good.
TL: To put up with all this.
FJ: There's not much family life at home really. The hours we work, the days we work.

Larry Davis: If they were bootlegging today, I'd be right in the middle of it. I love to run the lake, and I would have been right in it. I know I would have. There's no doubt in my mind.

Just as laws prohibiting liquor in the twenties were seen as unjust, so too are many of the current fishing regulations seen as unfair to fishermen. Perhaps a better analogy is in the outlaw heroes of the depression; in legend, "Pretty Boy" Floyd and Bonnie and Clyde, and in literature, Tom Joad in *The Grapes of Wrath* all became outlaws because of desperate economic times. Frank Jones and Sam Barnes are desperate; they see their choice as being outlaws or losing their boats and thus their means of making a living.

More common than the outlaw stories were ones in which a fisherman was arrested and used legal means to get off. Alva Snell had a story about attempting to outsmart a warden, getting caught, and ultimately winning in court.

PM: Generally were they fair to deal with or were there some problems down through the years?
AS: After all, that was their job. Once in awhile, you would kind of think maybe they came on a little too hard, but after all it was their job. I remember some of the last fishing I had done, I was on a gill-net boat down here at Kishman's, and we were fishing down almost to Lorain on the outside aways. We were just getting a lot of fish that were just under the margin. Had to measure them all cause it was so close to it, and we was laying there anchored, and picking fish out of the nets, you know. And I said, "Gee, those are nice fish to throw away. I think I'll take a nice mess of them home." I started throwing them in a box, and somebody else said, "Yes, save me a mess, too." Next thing you know everybody in the boat thought they ought to have a mess, and so we throwed them all in a box so we could clean them on the way home, and get them in their dinner buckets when we got in, so nobody would see us, you know. Somebody looked up and there was a state boat coming right at us, and it was getting right close. Gee, I jumped up quick and put this box had these small fish in it and dumped them over the side of the boat on the opposite side, you know, so they couldn't see it. They was coming from the other end. Dumped them overboard, see. They pulled up and tied up and got on the boat, and I started measuring the nets and looking at the fish, and of course, these fish that I had throwed overboard, part of them were dead. Being out of the net, they are a little different, and they started to drift where we was anchored, drift up from behind the boat. And one of them fellows seen it, and oh boy. He jumped into the boat, you know, and he had a dip net and he started to bail them fish out of there. The other fellow stayed on the boat.

There was two of them. Well, the fellow on the boat, he called in. Of course, they had the means to call Sandusky. Time we got into the dock out here at Kishman's, of course, there was four, and they took all our fish.

Had to go down to Lorain for the hearing. Of course, we was fishing down off Lorain. That's where they took it, to court down there. Ray [Full] hired a lawyer down there, and he come and had a talk with us before we had the hearing, so we learned a few things, you know, that we didn't know about what was going on. So we had the hearing, of course, and this lawyer got up and he says, "Any other boats in the vicinity?" "Oh, yes, there were other boats around." He says, "How do they know those fish were yours? Maybe they was somebody else's that drifted there. Got a mark on them some way to tell they was yours?" "Well, no." Oh gee, the wardens got so mad. That lawyer was so smart. He could do things, and he knew how to. So, finally, the judge says, "Where's the fish?" Do you know they had done something to those fish, either sold them or ate them or something, so they couldn't produce them, and the judge threw the thing out of court, and you know when we went out in the hall, of course, there were a lot of people there because a lot of them knew us, you know, and they was all there to find out about it. The warden was there, and he said, "I'm gonna show them God damn fishermen every time I get a chance." He was mad because he got beat. He knew, in a way, that we was at fault. You're not supposed to take small fish, but we was only taking enough for us for ourselves, you know. It wasn't like we was going to take a hundred pounds in and sell them, but nonetheless, when he seen them drifting by, he went wild.

This is another story that views the fishermen somewhat as outlaws; taking fish home for personal use is forbidden by law, but it is a common practice for fishermen. They see the law as unjust and therefore feel no compunctions about breaking it. In this case, the outlaw when caught uses the law to go free. Part of the satisfaction for fishermen in this story is using the warden's own laws against him, and as in several other stories the wardens are seen as not too bright.

Dean Koch of Castalia, one of the most politically outspoken active fishermen on western Lake Erie, told a story similar to Alva Snell's in which the fisherman's lawyer wins the case. The difference is that Koch saw his arrest as unjustified. The story is long and involved because it emphasizes technical legal details to prove his innocence. In the end the judge dismisses the case, and Koch comments, "Now, I don't like being harrassed. I don't like being arrested. I don't like bullshit arrests." Most fishermen told warden stories in which the arrest may have been justified by the law, but they felt the law itself was not just.

An unjust law was a central concern in comments made by Lewis Keller and Chester Jackson about the custom of bringing home fish in lunch buckets.

LK: Like I always said, when I fished for Lay Brothers out of Sandusky there, whenever they [the game wardens] wanted to put a fish fry on, they would go through all the boats when they come in and took the dinner buckets. Every dinner bucket would be loaded with fish. We used to get madder than hell at them, but we couldn't do nothing. They would just take the fish. They wouldn't arrest us or nothing. They just confiscated the fish. Then the next night or two, you'd see where they had a big fish fry.

CJ: If you had some nice twelve and a halves [inches] and you wanted a mess of pickerel and you wanted to take the twelve and a halves and leave the thirteens for the truck man, see for your own private use, nobody would say anything, you know, because there was so many out there.
PM: So back then it was fairly regular practice to take a few home.
CJ: Yes, no problem. That's one thing; if your pay wasn't good, you got all the fish you could eat. It's a slogan the boys had in town, you know. That might be good for your article. "The pay wasn't so good, but you got all the fish you could eat." That's the truth because that's what they used to throw at you, you know.

Keller's statement, "We used to get madder than hell at them, but we couldn't do nothing," encapsulates the attitude commercial fishermen had toward wardens, suggesting one of the reasons there are so many stories about wardens. Fishermen can express their hostility verbally even though they cannot express it any other way. Jackson's statement indicates that fishermen thought that taking fish home was their right, a fringe benefit to make up for low pay.

Keeping undersized fish was one of the major causes for arrest, but here again fishermen tell stories about beating the system.

Martin Hosko: And I tell you one of them was they changed the law the size of the perch. The law was eight and a half [inch] perch it had to be. An eight and a half inch fish was supposed to have a certain size fillet. Now they changed the size of the fillet to bigger size, so they could have an eight and a half inch perch, and whenever they filleted it, the fillet may not, if the men wasn't careful cutting it by the hair. You made a short fillet out of a legal size fish. And I fought it, and I took it to court, and I won. I'm right. I had legal fish. The law says eight and a half inch perch, but the woman or the man that cut them wasn't careful cutting the head off, cut it a little short, he made a short fillet out of a legal size fish. And they made the arrest on that, and by God, I took them to court, and I fought them. They got beat on that one.

As a prominent fish house owner, Martin Hosko not only had contact with wardens but also with administrators in state agencies and with members of the Wildlife Council. His attitudes are the same as other fishermen, but the experiences on which they are based are wider. After he served a term on the Wildlife Council, Hosko believed that policymakers were ignorant about fish. According to Hosko, the people of the Wildlife Council do not even know the difference among the fish species that they are regulating.

So Jim Sikes [chairman of the Wildlife Council; not his real name] says to me, he says, "Marty," he says, "What's the walleyes the chief telling us is so scarce?" . . . And, Bob, I had about fifty pounds of them on the truck ready to push overboard. I was picking out the perch, white bass that was involved. He says, "Marty, what does walleyes the chief's telling us is so scarce [look like]?" "Well," I says, "Ed, this is walleyes." I give them a push. I says, "That's fifty dollars overboard." "You kidding?" So I bailed out another couple nets full. I had another fifty pounds, so they counted. We had six hundred fish. . . . Jim Sikes says to me, he says, "You know, Marty, I don't know one fish from another." But he was the chairman. . . . That's our Wildlife Council. That's what's making commercial fishermen lost.

All of the stories about wardens and the enforcement of laws picture commercial fishermen as essentially moral independent businessmen trying to make a living who must sometimes break the laws because the laws are unjust. The wardens and others who enforce the laws are viewed as ignorant of the actual conditions on the lake. Thus the in-group self-image of fishermen comes about at least partially in opposition to another group and involves both their image of themselves and what they think others think of them.

Most commercial fishermen believe that a political coalition of sport fishermen, tackle manufacturers, and state legislators is responsible for the stricter regulations, and that wardens apply the laws more aggressively to commercial than to sport fishermen. Lewis Keller repeated his opinions about sport fishermen several times in the interviews.

> You take the game wardens today, I don't know, it's your sport fishermen that's taking over, and the game wardens are right with them. That's the only thing I can say. It ain't nothing like it used to be years ago. Years ago you would catch a few undersized fish and that; they didn't bother you much. Jesus, today, man, they catch you for every little damn thing. I think some of these guys would arrest their own grandmother if they caught them. They just, I don't know, it's just the way life is. But that's your sportsman.

> But everybody's got it in their head today that the commercial fisherman, it's drilled in their heads, it's been in the papers and everything else where your commercial fishermen are catching everything, fishing the lake out. Well, that's not true. That's the way the sportsmen has got it. They got it built up, and they got big pieces of paper, and they say the commercial fishermen are killing off all the fish. They're catching them all, and the lake is going to hell, you know. They don't come out and tell what really the truth is about your pollution and your fish feed.

Keller speaks for most commercial fishermen when he sees a conspiracy among sport fishermen and wardens to blame commercial fishermen for everything wrong in the lake. Part of his bias against sport fishermen is based on class distinctions.

> That's what I said, it's not right. It's not treating the commercial fishermen right. These outdoorsmen, as I call them, they are a bunch of hothead millionaires. They've got dough and this and that, and they are going to do the way they want regardless. You can't tell them nothing. When you try to tell them that they are all wrong, oh no, that's out. But you take me, now I've been on the water now, well, ever since, well, I was born and raised on it you might as well say.

The same sort of oppositional identity that occurs in the warden stories can be seen in this comment by Keller: the rich sport fishermen are contrasted to the working-class commercial fishermen thereby enhancing the positive identity of Keller and his co-workers. He feels that being born and raised on the water gives him certain rights over the wealthy newcomers to Lake Erie. They are seen as interlopers in his domain. Keller's view is an extreme one, but other fishermen feel this way to a lesser degree.

Keller comes into contact with sport fishermen and argues with them but has been unable to convince them of his point of view.

PM: When you're down at Turinsky's sitting around in the mornings like you say you do sometimes, down at Turinsky's Docks, do you ever get an opportunity to tell the sport fishermen your point of view?

LK: Oh, you, we tell them, but they don't understand what you're talking about. They don't know what the hell a commercial fisherman's life is all about. They just think they'll believe these other guys, and tell you no, they're catching all the fish and this and that. But they never say anything when they go out hook-and-line fishing and bring in little perch that big and little pickerel that big [indicates a very small fish with his fingers].

His description of direct contact with sport fishermen sets up a situation of differential identity (Bauman 1971) in which a person's identity is formed based on his differences with others. This is not exactly the same as oppositional identity because it depends on an actual context in which there is interaction between the two groups, and opposition can occur without this. Perhaps Keller's interaction within a differential context explains why he has such a strong and definite identity as a fisherman. His frequent contact with sport fishermen reminds him through contrast who he is, and he feels the need to project that identity because he is aware of the negative view they have of him.

Alva Snell's interaction with sport fishermen has also convinced him that most are not knowledgeable about fish.

I'm in arguments all the time down there cleaning fish for the hook-and-line fishermen. You can't believe the foolish things that they will come in and say. They complain about commercial fishermen, and they don't know what they are talking about or not. And what gets me, being a commercial fisherman all my life, they will come in with perch that long [indicates three or four inches] and curse the commercial fisherman for catching all the big ones and just leaving in the small ones. And here they are, they are killing off the little fish that never spawned. . . . But they don't think they are hurting the fishing any, you know. Oh, no, it's all right; it's the goddamn commercial fisherman who's got all them big ones. And it burns me up. I mean fair is fair, but they can't see it. They think they should have all the lake. I think the commercial fisherman has been hurt by the hook-and-line fishermen that follow fishing.

Snell, like Keller, is in a situation of differential identity, and he also has a more defiant identity as a commercial fisherman to project because of this context. He has to listen to sport fishermen criticize commercial fishermen, and he feels a need to respond.

The currently active commercial fishermen observe the same kind of ignorance in sport fishermen's behavior.

Joe Herr: You see them come in here with perch that're three or four inches long, and not one or two [of them]. I'm talking a cooler full, and not one guy, but almost everybody that comes through there with their little coolers.

Paul Leidorf: In September and October, and they got little bitty baby perch like that in there, and you can't—

JH: They said, "There ain't no big fish out there cause the God damn fishermen caught them all. Lousy, rotten commercial fishermen, let's go sink one of their boats."

PL: Then said, "I'll tell you what; you ought to be ashamed of yourself."

JH: I said, "I wouldn't carry something like that [a very small fish] through the door. I'd hide. You should go in the corner and duck your head. You should be totally ashamed of doing something like killing a baby like that. What are you going to do with it? All you got is flavored skin; you can't eat the damn thing."

PM: No meat on it.

JH: They said, "Where are all the big ones?" I said, "If you didn't catch all the damn small ones, there would be some big ones. You know you can't have big ones unless you got small ones too." Dumb son-of-a-bitches, boy. Don't get me going. I get mad.

There is extreme oppositional identity here: Herr and Leidorf portray sport and commercial fishermen as absolute opposites. They use sarcasm to undermine the sport fishermen's view of them, "Lousy, rotten commercial fishermen," while it is clear that this is actually the commercial fishermen's view of the sport fishermen, the "dumb son-of-a-bitches."

Herr and Leidorf encounter sport fishermen every day, which means that differential and oppositional identity are both affecting them. There is hostility on both sides.

JH: [A commercial fishing] boat got hit by a pleasure boat some-time last night. Bent it so the tail gate don't fit no more.
PM: And whoever hit it just kept on going?
JH: It's only a fisherman. What the hell do you stop for? Scum of the earth, you know. Second-class citizen. Till they break down out there and want you to tow them in.
PM: Then you're all right?
JH: I'm not. I get the radio out and call the Coast Guard.
PM: You won't tow them, huh?
JH: I used to all the time. Go out of my way. I towed one guy from three miles out . . . hell, within a half mile of the river, and he says, "Oh, I got her fixed." Untied the line, and away he went. He was just a little low on gas is all. He didn't go on the river, he went that way. I couldn't catch him. About a twenty foot inboard-outboard. No way. So I just come in and tied up, and I said that is absolutely the last one. Never again. And I've never towed one since. I call the Coast Guard for them. Do you know what the Coast Guard told them? Float. Simple as that. No respect whatsoever for them.

Herr also told a comic story that clearly expressed his contempt for sport fishermen.

You heard about that, didn't you? Them guys [sport fishermen] were out there in the golf course that runs up past Huron, teed off, and looked and there was this great big fish in the creek right there. Water's only that deep. Took their golf club and they're beating them with their golf clubs. Somebody seen them. Got arrested for it. It's not sportsmanlike to club a salmon with a golf club.

Herr's opinion of sport fishermen is similar to Lewis Keller's; part of the hostility they feel is a result of class resentment. The golfing fisherman fits Herr's stereotype of the wealthy sportsman who has a lot of leisure time in which to do stupid things in contrast to the hard-working commercial fisherman whose only pleasure, as Alva Snell suggests, is in his work.

Commercial fishermen seem to view pleasure boats and sport fishing boats as one category: they both belong to wealthy people who care little for the rights of commercial fishing boats. Alva Snell towed several pleasure boats in during his years of fishing, and although in a couple of cases he was thanked and rewarded, he vividly remembers one unpleasant encounter.

Well, sometimes you get kind of like a yacht broke down out there, and I went out to it, and I told the fellows I was fishing out of Lorain. I was going back to Lorain. Well, he says, "Couldn't you tow us into Cleveland?" I said, "No, that's too far out of our way. We'd be late getting in, and the outfit we work for would figure something is wrong. They would be sending a boat out or something." We would usually get in about a certain time. I said, "I'll take you to Lorain if you want to go." "Well, okay." If they had to, they had to. Well, I knew they had been drinking. I could tell by the way they was acting. One fellow got up on the nose of the yacht, you know, and they fastened a line there and made everything look good. So we got all ready to go. I said, "Go on, get back down in the boat." "I'm all right; go ahead, go ahead," he says. Well, I started ahead real easy. I figured, sure enough, just as soon as that line tightened up, overboard he went, had to go back.

He had a great big paunch on him. He was drunk. Tried to get him into the boat, and we could not get him. That boat's got what you call a fender streak. You know, it runs all the way around the edge of the boat to keep them away from the dock and one thing or another. So, we tried and tried. Finally, I said to the other fellows in the boat, "You pull up on his arms, and I'll reach overboard and get one of his legs. Maybe we can roll him in like we would a pig." And all the time the fella was saying, "I'm done for, I'm done for, I'm done for." And finally, we rolled him down into the bottom of the fish motor, and he laid there and rolled around like a big pig. Down dirty in the fish and tar and dust and everything on the bottom of a fish boat. He said, "I'm done for, I'm done for." "You're all right. Shut up."

So we got into the dock. I think we put him back in his own boat, if I remember right. Pulled him into the fish dock, got in. He come over with a bottle of booze and wanted to give it to us for pay for helping him. I says, "Hey, buddy, you had no business out in the boat, and you see what happened. It's your damn fault. Just take your booze and go on." I felt a little bit disgusted by it. We had worked overtime to get him in there, and then give us a bottle of booze. Here he pert near drowned.

Snell seems to get a great deal of pleasure out of telling this story, and oppositional identity helps to explain why. In the narrative the yachtsman and the commercial fisherman have exchanged roles: the yachtsman fulfills the negative stereotype of the fisherman—he is drunk and wallowing in the smelly fish—and the fisherman is the opposite—a clean, nondrinking competent person in charge of the situation. Anytime a fisherman can tell a story in which his behavior is so positively contrasted to an opposing group, then he has to feel satisfaction in the telling.

Throughout these conflict stories, whether with wardens, sport fishermen, or other groups, commercial fishermen project a positive image of themselves in contrast to negative views of their perceived enemies. Opposition with other groups and differential situations in which they interact with outsiders are significant elements in shaping their occupational identity. From what retired fishermen say, these have always been factors in the formation of identity, but in the last thirty years, conflict and opposition have become even more important in making fishermen who they are. They have evolved even stronger identities because they see themselves on the brink of extinction.

Commercial fishermen are clearly pessimistic about their occupational future on Lake Erie. They do not feel they have enough political clout to remedy their situation.

PM: Do you guys have a lobbying group in Columbus? Do you have an organization to—?
Joe Herr: We got an organization, but there ain't enough of us to do anything.
PM: Yes, it takes numbers to really get some pull.
Paul Leidorf: It takes numbers and money, and there's no money there.
PM: The sport fishermen have the money and the numbers.
PL: I'm so damn poor they can't pay any attention.
PM: That's really bad.
JH: So we've been getting the shaft for about the last ten years.
PL: It's been coming a long time.
JH: When they first started all this shit, there was a pretty active

commercial fisherman, and there must have been all the way up and down the lake probably four thousand fished a day, trap nets.

PL: Lay Brothers used to put eight hundred or so out a year.

JH: Just out of this building they would take eight hundred nets.

PL: Now lakewide I think the last count was two hundred thirty nets fished. Last year.

JH: Last year. Now, this year, there's like Marky Zimmerman, he's gone. Hanks is gone. Andy's gone. You know, I think it's down to about two hundred thirty nets now, lake wide in Ohio.

Dean Koch has a pair of solutions to the problem. The first would institute a new system of licensing and recordkeeping for sport fishermen, which would theoretically increase income to the state. The second calls for a state buyout of commercial fishing operations, followed by (Koch believes) the state's realization of the value of a healthy commercial fishing industry and the re-establishment of commercial fishing on what he feels is a more reasonable economic and political basis. Thus far, he has not been able to interest the state in either part of his plan.

Unless some new plan or regulatory system is put into place, it seems clear that the commercial fishing industry on Ohio's Lake Erie waters will come to an end during the next decade. Without the living occupation to create and support it, the occupational culture—knowledge, technique, custom, and narrative—will also soon disappear, first from active use and then from memory.

Conclusion: Personal Narratives and Occupational Identity

A fisherman talking about his work tends to make his occupational life into a series of stories, and those stories reveal who he thinks he is. His personal experiences are unique, but he also shares certain experiences with other fishermen. The identity projected in the narratives, then, will be both personal and social. For instance, Alva Snell had run-ins with yachtsmen that are unlike the experiences of any other fishermen, but like most fishermen we interviewed, he has tried factory work and eventually returned to fishing. His story about his factory experience shares a basic theme and patterns with other fishermen's stories of like events. Fishermen's narratives project not a single identity but multiple personal and social identities.

Folklore is a key to understanding these many identities because fishermen, like members of any occupational group, use their stories to shape and express identities. As folklorist Alan Dundes points out, "Not only does folklore serve as a kind of autobiographical ethnography, a mirror made by the people themselves, which reflects a group's identity, but it also represents valuable data which is relatively free from the outside observer's bias" (Dundes 1983, 259). The situation with fishermen is more complex than Dundes's conception suggests; fishermen reveal themselves as they tell their own stories, but the resulting data is not relatively free from the outsider's bias. The fishermen are very much aware of projecting an image to the outside because they are so conscious of what outsiders think of them. In many ways fishermen's narratives actually reflect the outsider's bias, but it has been turned around, inverted at times, in order to project a positive image of fishermen. Also, we must consider ourselves—folklorists—

as outside observers with our own biases, which also affect the presentation of self through narrating.

Besides being multiple, then, identities are often oppositional; that is, one group forms its identity partially on the basis of differences with other groups, not just on shared values within the group (Spicer 1971, 797). This can be seen in the stories fishermen tell about conflicts with wardens and sport fishermen (chapter 6). Each fisherman's story of conflict is thematically like the others, but the details emphasized and the attitudes expressed vary from story to story. Some personal occupational narratives are based on the oppositional principle and at the same time reflect multiple identities.

The scholarship on identity covers a broad range of disciplines, including psychoanalysis, social psychology, anthropology, ethnic studies, and education, but except for ethnic studies, scholars have ignored the role of folklore in the expression of identity. Folklore studies, on the other hand, have concentrated on ethnicity as a defining factor in determining identity, but with some notable exceptions, folklorists have not dealt much with other influences such as occupation, age, social status, and so forth. Identity is such a complex concept that definitions from various disciplines must be taken into account when applying it to folklore. Erik Erikson was one of the first scholars to study identity in depth, and his definitions contain many of the central concepts still being analyzed. Erikson states, "The term identity expresses . . . a mutual relation in that it connotes both a persistent sameness within oneself (selfsameness) and a peristent sharing of some kind of essential character with others" (1959, 102). A continuing paradox in the scholarship is suggested here: the concept of "self" implies distinctiveness while at the same time sameness is necessary for identity. A group or an individual can be both distinctive with respect to other groups or individuals and have sameness in terms of continuity over time (Jacobson-Widding 1983, 13). Commercial fishermen have a distinctive group identity that has remained relatively the same over a period of years, and each individual fisherman has his own personal identity as a distinct member of the group that lasts, with some variation, a lifetime.

Identity is not static, though. It changes with the life cycle (Erikson 1959, 50–100). A core identity may remain the same, but variations occur through life experiences. For instance, the choice of occupation by a young person is a crucial identity-forming decision (Erikson 1959,

92), but a person may change occupations several times during her or his life. After an occupational identity has been chosen, it is still subject to influence and change from other forces and therefore must be analyzed as it relates to other kinds of identity, both personal and social. Anthropologists such as Ward Goodenough have studied the dynamic impact that social change has on identity; in this regard he says, "Any change that affects the existing social order or a person's ability to conduct himself in accordance with it must also affect his identity and sense of worth" (1963, 177). A person can change from one job to another, or the public perception of a particular kind of work can shift. As many of the preceding stories have indicated, the public perception of commercial fishermen is an important factor in shaping fishermen's identity.

The importance of both the self and others in identity formation (Erikson 1959, 102) suggests the interrelatedness of individual and group identity. Identity is made up of social components such as class and ethnicity and of individual components such as personality traits and behavioral attributes (Liebkind 1983, 187; Zavalloni 1973). The social and the personal are interdependent; personality traits, for example, are partially based on such social factors as class and ethnicity. In order to study the multiple nature of identity, one must look not just at the individual or the group but at *both*. Dundes has reviewed the scholarship on identity and has commented:

> The bulk of identity scholarship has tended to focus either on the self or on the group, especially the ethnic group. There can be no question that self-identity or personal identity is a legitimate subject for any serious theoretical treatment of identity, but, by the same token, it is a great over-simplification to limit discussions of identity to "self." Similarly, important as ethnic identity may be, it is only one type of identity, that is one type of group identity (1983, 241).

Personal experience narratives can convey many sorts of identity at once. When a fisherman tells of a work experience, the story not only reflects his occupational identity, it also contain signs of his personality, ethnicity, religious beliefs, and more. For example, Alva Snell has a strong sense of family that is related to his occupational identity because his father and grandfather were fishermen. A particular story he tells can project occupational, family, and religious concerns at the same time. In performance terms, multiplicity can be seen when an individual tells a story within a group context. Each fisherman has a personal identity that is reflected in his stories along with the occupational identity he shares with others. When Paul Leidorf and Joe Herr talk about their job experiences together, two distinctive personalities emerge, but a shared sense of themselves as fishermen also comes out. In much the same way, according to Jack Santino, the personal storytelling of Pullman porters is both a "presentation of personal identity and an arena in which personal identity is negotiated by the group. Both personal and cultural perspectives are provided" (1983, 410). The personal experience narrative can be a private rather than a communal expression, especially within such contexts as the family (Dolby-Stahl 1985, 48), but within an occupational context the personal story becomes more communal and less intimate. Fishermen telling stories to other fishermen or to folklorists will not need to create intimacy to the same degree that a mother telling a personal story to a daughter will (Dolby-Stahl 1985).

The personal side of identity is stressed in "life story" studies, and personal occupational narratives can be viewed as episodes in a life story. Jeff Todd Titon points out that the "life story's singular achievement is that it affirms the identity of the storyteller in the act of the telling. The life story tells who one thinks one is and how one thinks one came to be that way" (1980, 290). To shape one's identity through the telling of personal narratives, a person selects those experiences from his or her life in which symbolic value can be discerned. For instance, a fisherman will choose occupational experiences that will communicate what he and other fishermen think are significant events. A fisherman may repeat a story of a near miss with a freighter but not one about a hole in his net because the self-image he wants to project is partially based on the danger but not the mundane details of his work. Everyday nuisances are part of the work and hence part of occupational identity, but these will not necessarily be communicated to others. When a fisherman tells of significant incidents in his occupational life he is affirming his personal identity in terms of his job, and each man's story is different in some way so that the basis for multiple identities within one group is established.

Such characteristics as "nationality, sex, social class, profession, age group, family situation, political orientation, and ethnic and religious origin" make up social identity (Zavalloni 1983, 286), and these features must be considered in analyzing the role of personal narrative in projecting self-image. Several such features help to determine identity for commercial fishermen, including the fisherman's age and the corresponding stage of his occupational life, his social and economic class, his family background, his personal traits, and his religious, ethnic, and family values from outside the occupation. These features are not uniformly distributed among the fishermen we interviewed; for some, family is important as it relates to occupation, for others it has no bearing; for only one man, Martin Hosko, was ethnicity a meaningful feature. Also, not all of these features are articulated as significant by the fishermen: Lewis Keller might not ever mention class distinctions as being important to him, but his remark about sport fishermen as "hothead millionaires" reveals his class resentments. No one specifically said that Jib Snyder was lower class or John Lay was upper class, but the stories about them make their social level a determining factor for the purpose of the story. Thus these are etic categories (determined by scholarly analysis), but internal evidence gives emic (native) support for them (Dundes 1962; Pike 1954–60).

The context of performance also influences the projection of identity. An individual talker may alter his presentation of identity depending on the situation he is in: telling occupational stories within a family context is not the same as within a workplace context or in an interview situation. For example, an obscene story that projects a culturally defined masculine identity might be appropriate in the workplace but obviously not at a family picnic unless the language is changed. Other situations have corresponding shifts of identity and altering of style and repertoire. Occupational contexts do not simply influence expressions, they are a part of the interaction itself (McCarl 1978, 146).

A fisherman's age is an important determinant of identity: a retired fisherman will not express the same self-image as one just starting out. Here again there is internal evidence for this as a recognized category of narrative by the fishermen: retired fishermen used rhetorical devices such as repeated phrases—"in those days," "years ago," and others—to frame their stories as being set in the past and to project themselves as knowledgeable spokesmen about the old days. Younger, still active fishermen did not use these devices, but they may use them later after their own retirement. Thus identity is flexible and changes during the life cycle (Dundes 1983, 243). One entire category of occupational personal narrative was told mainly by retired fishermen; only rarely did an active older fisherman tell "golden age" stories, and no younger men told any. Jack Santino was the first folklorist to identify this pattern: "Every industry's workers seem to have a conception of a golden age, a time before the present when things were different or somehow better" (1978, 204). Among fishermen these stories are told only by men who are projecting an identity as elders, ones who see themselves as removed from the way things are now. When they were active, they say, there were more fish and there was less pollution; men were better, they worked longer and harder but liked the work. In other words, not only the age, but also the men who worked in it were "golden." Eighty-six-year-old Bob Bodi went so far as to say, "There's no good fishermen anymore" (chapter 2). Identity in this case is based on an idealized past; the storytellers are older, but they also consider themselves better than fishermen today.

Fishermen come from several different social and economic classes, from deckhands to fish company owners, and these class identities were revealed in the stories fishermen told. Martin Hosko owned a fish house in Toledo; Bob Bodi worked on one of Hosko's boats for twenty-one years. Hosko's stories emphasized what a fair boss he was; for instance, he told a story about a retarded man he employed out of kindness. Bodi's stories showed his concern for doing physical tasks well, reflecting his pride in a job well done: "On a nice day, I think the most enjoyment I ever got out of life was to see that string of twine setting there perfect like that." Hosko then commented, "And it done the same thing to me, Bob. It sort of thrilled me more than you because it was mine" (chapter 1). The deckhand's identity is based on his work; the boss's on his ownership.

The character anecdotes fishermen told can also be classified as personal narratives because most were based on personal contact with the eccentrics or notable men being described. Many similar narratives are told about individual characters in local fishermen's tradition, and these characters should be seen as symbolic representatives of the group as well as individual protagonists in actual situations (Santino 1978, 208). In the character stories we can discern different identities formed by the fishermen's own distinctions about class. The "lower class" of fishermen was represented by Jib Snyder of Vermilion, a filthy alcoholic who was described in this way: "But he was dirty. Oh, stink! You could smell him a block away" (chapter 3). The responsible, "middle-class" fisherman was symbolized by the hard-working strong man Ed Lampe, who while carrying two hundred pounds of lead weights across a bridge stopped to have a conversation in the middle without ever putting down the weights (chapter 3). The representative "upper-class" character was "Old John" Lay who owned Lay Brothers Fisheries in Sandusky, "the largest independent fishery in the world, not just the United States, in the world, at that time." Stories about him revolve around how "good-hearted" he was, how he worked alongside his men, provided them bonuses, and gave free fish to poor people and widows in town (chapter 3). The stories of and about Clifford Baker, the Prohibition rumrunner, show his membership in both the "middle" and "upper" classes. He had the skill, intuition, and cunning admired by fishermen (even when it was evidenced through illegal activities); he was a responsible and hard-working man; and he was equally well known for his efficient and clean operation of a successful fishing business and his fairness to employees. The men who told these stories identified with the characters in them to one degree or another, except, of course, with Jib Snyder. The stories about him were a means of dealing with some of the negative stereotypes of fishermen held by outsiders (Mullen 1978b, 113–29). By laughing at Jib Snyder stories, they could disassociate themselves from the stereotype.

Family background was another basis for personal identity. Fishermen whose fathers and grandfathers were also fishermen told "starting-out" stories that emphasized the roles their fathers had in getting them into the fishing business (Santino 1978, 204). Alva Snell and Lewis Keller narrated lengthy incidents in which their fathers were instrumental in them becoming fishermen (chapter 2). Alva Snell indicated the importance of family with a rhetorical device that presented his lineage as a litany: "my father was a commercial fisherman, my grandfather was a commercial fisherman, my great-grandfather was a commercial fisherman. . . ." He did not have to use this parallel structure here, but it helps to frame his story of how he got started in fishing within the continuum of family history. Family identity was linked to occupational identity in these instances, but many fishermen lacked this connection, and their starting-out stories had a variety of identity features. Martin Hosko's story was an immigrant experience narrative, because he had come from Czechoslovakia to the United States to work (chapter 2). Luke Gowitzka's starting-out narrative told how a dream influenced him to become a fisherman; his was the only story that contained a supernatural element, culturally based to be sure, but not part of the usual occupational self-image of fishermen and thus an example of personal traits as a basis for identity (chapter 2). Bob Bodi's focus on neat work might seem to be a shared occupational trait, but in fact he and his boss Martin Hosko were the only ones we interviewed who emphasized this (chapters 1 and 5).

The value placed on hard work is widely shared, but Chester Jackson and Alva Snell placed such a great emphasis on it in their stories and conversation that it seems more closely tied to the larger cultural value of the Protestant work ethic, which seems to have influenced them personally more than it did other fishermen. Jackson proudly tells of being nicknamed "Slavedriver" Jackson because he worked so hard and expected his men to do the same. Snell tells the following story of how hard he worked before he retired.

> Tell you another funny thing that happened, you know. Years ago, as I told you, you worked seven days a week, and there was no eight-hour day like there is now. In fact, I joined what they called the trap netters' union at one time. There was lots of fishermen at that time, and the contract called for ten-hour days, eleven hours in the spring and fall when you was setting and pulling the nets, to get them out of the lake or something. But you worked ten hours a day and didn't think anything of it. Finally, got to a nine-hour day. Finally down to eight. Well, I was out in the lake and just started with an eight-hour day, and looked at my watch, and said, "Oh, my gosh, the day is—we gotta get started for home. We're going to be working overtime." And one of the fellas said, "I've never seen anything like it." He says, "I can stand on my head eight hours." Other fella in the boat says, "Why, I can hold my breath for that long." It seemed so short after working for ten hours to work for eight (chapter 2).

This story, of course, also fits into the "we were better men back then" category; it illustrates how a shared group trait is combined with a personal one in a particular story. However, not all of the different types of stories express multiple identities. The "close call" narratives (chapter 4), which are analogous to stories told by firefighters (McCarl 1985, 154), all have the same themes with little or no individual variation; they emphasize the hazards of the job and the determination of the men to go out no matter what risks have to be faced.

The existence of multiple identities within a body of occupational narratives indicates the importance of individual personality in storytelling, even within a group context. In this, the personal occupational narrative is similar to the life story. Titon makes a significant point when he says, "Personality is the main ingredient in the life story. It is a fiction, just like the story; and even if the story is not factually true, it is always true evidence of the storyteller's personality" (1980, 290). Fiction in this sense does not necessarily mean untrue, but something created, an artistic expression, which many of the fishermen's stories certainly are (Dolby-Stahl 1985, 54; Leary 1984, 43). Part of the creative act in narrating these stories is the blending of individual and group concerns, making the story immediate through personal involvement and making it relevant through the expression of shared traits.

The other important principle in forming and maintaining identities in personal occupational narrative is oppositional dynamics (Spicer 1971, 797). The concept of oppositional identity is not based on similarities within the group, but on differences with other groups. Folklorist Richard Bauman uses a similar term, *differential identity*, to characterize specific performance contexts: "difference of identity, not necessarily sharing, can be at the base of folklore performance," and "members of particular groups or social categories may exchange folklore with each other, on the basis of shared identity, or with others, on the basis of differential identity" (1971, 35, 38). Through many of their narratives fishermen define themselves in opposition to several other groups, including land-based occupations, game wardens, sport fishermen, and the general population, which has many negative stereotypes of fishermen. Differential identity is part of the performance of their stories in several situations, especially in their contact with newspaper reporters, television interviewers, sport fishermen, and folklorists.

The most pervasive pattern in the personal narratives of fishermen on western Lake Erie is one in which a fisherman quits his job on the water, takes a factory job, becomes disgusted with it, quits, and returns to fishing in the lake. We have called these "in your blood" stories because fishermen often use that or similar phrases to explain why they continue in their occupation despite hard work, long hours, low pay, and governmental restrictions. Paul Leidorf told a brief version of this sort of story.

> I've had good jobs, and I've had enough education that I could [make a] go in it. I've been in like . . . bearings and working on transmissions. I hated that so bad. I knew how many steps it took

to get there, and it didn't take as many steps to get out, cause they were a little bit longer. There's just something about it. I basically spent my life, you might say, on the lake (chapter 5).

Clearly stories of this kind project identity based on opposition: the identity of fishermen as independent, freedom-loving outdoorsmen is made apparent by contrast with the time-clock bound, subordinate, indoor life of the factory worker as perceived by fishermen. This clear-cut identity would not exist without another group to provide a contrast.

Other groups that fishermen come in contact with also provide the basis for oppositional identity. Fishermen often tell stories about game wardens and sport fishermen, who they see as their adversaries. The wardens enforce what the fishermen think of as unfair regulations that make it difficult to realize a profit, and in the fishermen's minds sport fishermen have combined with tackle manufacturers to form a strong lobby for legislation to outlaw all commercial fishing on the American side of the lake. The stories about wardens and sport fishermen stress their stupidity—they cannot tell one species of fish from another, for instance—and are often about outwitting a game warden (chapter 6). These stories are similar to the "authority stories" collected by Tim Cochrane from commercial fishermen on Isle Royale in Lake Superior: "authority stories are built upon a conceptual polarization of two groups [by asserting that] rangers' and wardens' actions are wrong, thus fishermen's [actions] are right" (1983). The fishermen project a self-image of intelligence and knowledge in contrast to the ignorance and stupidity of wardens and sport fishermen.

Just as fishermen negatively stereotype game wardens and sport fishermen, they also have to contend with negative stereotypes of them held by the surrounding population. Much of folklore, in fact, is formed to create or counteract such stereotypes. As Dundes says, "It could well be argued that one of the most important links between folklore and identity has to do with stereotypes. The distinctive, character trait of any identity set—no matter whether the set is based on sex, nationality, ethnicity, religious affiliation, occupation, etc.—is very probably the subject (or object) of stereotyping" (1983, 250).

Negative stereotyping of fishermen is widespread: they are generally viewed as poor, uneducated, dirty, and alcoholic (Gilmore 1983). From our observation these stereotypes are prevalent on the western Lake

Erie coast, and the fishermen themselves think that this is the way they are perceived by outsiders. What they think others think of them is basic to the situation necessary for oppositional identity (Jansen 1959). According to Robert McCarl, a similar pattern exists with firefighters: the outside negative stereotype of them as lazy and dumb is opposed in their occupational narratives by a positive in-group view (1985, 128–36).

Fishermen's narratives and comments reflect both sides of the image; the Jib Snyder narratives project the alcoholic identity, although the storytellers clearly distance themselves personally from this image. Several fishermen spoke directly of drinking as a social activity. Lewis Keller said, "All the fishermen drank. I don't give a damn who it was. Every Saturday afternoon we'd all end up in one big bar, and we'd drink beer till hell wouldn't have it" (chapter 5). Keller seems to link drinking with the fishermen's independence, but other fishermen had a different view. We asked Alva Snell what fishermen did for recreation, and he replied:

> Well, the natural thought when you speak of a fisherman is he's going to spend his spare time in a bar.
> **Tim Lloyd:** Is that true though?
> **Alva Snell:** Well, I didn't drink, and I didn't smoke, but I spent a lot of my spare time just traveling (chapter 5).

This discussion illustrates the oppositional principle at work: without us mentioning drinking, Snell brings up the stereotype of the drunken fisherman, an outsider's view that he might have suspected we held, which he then contrasts with his own identity as a nondrinker. Some fishermen drink, some do not: their narratives and commentary reveal multiple identities in response to the stereotyping of outsiders. Overall, their stories project the positive occupational identity of hard-working, independent, and freedom-loving men in opposition to such negative stereotypes.

Because fishermen are constantly aware of these negative images, the situations in which they perform their stories are often occasions for the expression of differential identity. Active commercial fishermen come into contact with sport fishermen and game wardens daily, and although fishermen do not tell dumb warden stories to the wardens, the contact is a reminder of differential identity. Several retired fishermen converse with outsiders regularly; Lewis Keller can often be found at the sportfishing dock in Marblehead talking about his fishing days, and Alva Snell runs a fish-cleaning business in Vermilion where he talks and tells stories to his sport fishermen customers. Both of these men project strong occupational identities in their stories, and this is at least partially explained by the dynamics of their interaction with outsiders; they feel a need to counter the negative view with which they come in contact.

Another significant performance situation determined by differential identity is the folklorists' interview with fishermen. Folklorists are perceived as sympathetic and interested representatives of the outside world, which is how we presented ourselves, and thus a means for the fisherman to communicate his point of view to that world. One of the storyteller's major goals in this situation is to project his own view to outsiders who have misunderstood him. Anytime a tape recorder or outside observer is known to be present by the performer, the situation becomes one of differential identity rather than of shared group identity, and storytelling style and repertoire are affected. The group dynamics of a tape-recorded storytelling session do not have the formality of an interview, but there is always an element of exoteric awareness of the outside as well as esoteric shared values (Jansen 1959). However, one situation is not more of a "natural context" and the other less; they are both natural because they involve performance of folklore in a specific recurring frame. Nessa Wolfson makes a point about the sociolinguistic interview that can be applied to folklore fieldwork: "The formal interview is . . . a recognized speech event in our society. Members of the society know the rules of speaking for interviews. They expect to be asked a series of questions and to answer them. Although being interviewed is hardly an everyday experience for most people, there is nothing 'artificial' or 'unnatural' about it" (1976, 195).

For many of the fishermen we interviewed, this was not their first time to be recorded. Alva Snell had been videotaped by students from nearby Oberlin College. Several men brought out newspaper clippings of previous stories written on them. We tape-recorded situations in which two fishermen talked and told stories to each other rather than in a formal interview, but in both cases the storytelling was based on their awareness of their different identities in opposition to ours and to the outside world. The fishermen were all aware of recent negative articles about commercial fishing in outdoor columns in area newspapers, and often told us that they saw the interview as their chance to offer their side of the story, to project a positive identity against the negative outside view. The personal experience narratives and occupational commentary of commercial fishermen on western Lake Erie are thus a symbolic manifestation of their struggle to maintain personal and occupational identities in the face of social changes that may be destroying the occupation itself.

In their concern for what outsiders think of them, commercial fishermen on Lake Erie are like fishermen and other occupational groups throughout the United States. Shrimpers in the Gulf of Mexico, salmon fishermen and tuna seiners in the Pacific, surfmen, baymen, and deepsea fishermen in the Atlantic, and fishermen in Lake Superior all have to face increased governmental regulation, hostility from sport fishermen, and steroryping by the general population (Cochrane 1983; Gilmore 1986; Matthiessen 1986; Mullen 1978b; Orbach 1977; Poggie and Gersuny 1974). In response to the increasing strength of these outside forces, Lake Erie fishermen have become even more insular and their occupational identity even more fixed. The same is true for other occupational groups that have to contend with this kind of misunderstanding from the outside; Pullman porters, firefighters, offshore oil drillers, and loggers are typical of occupations that have a strong in-group identity formed in opposition to outside views of them (Fields 1974; McCarl 1985; Santino 1983; Toelken 1979, 52–72). Loggers and oil-field workers confront many of the same problems as commercial fishermen; shrinking natural resources and growing concerns for the environment have placed restrictions on their activities and caused public opinion toward them to change. Technological change, population growth, and resulting problems such as pollution and declining resources continue to be a threat to fishermen and to other occupations. Thus Lake Erie fishermen are not unique; the investigation of their identity has application to other occupations. The present study is an attempt to gain a greater understanding of an occupational group from within by looking closely at their own stories and their self-images. Other works treat the larger environmental and political issues more thoroughly, but the workers' side of the story must also be considered in order to find fair and just solutions to these issues.

Glossary

Buoy: A float that indicates the end of a net as it sits in the water. Ohio commercial fishing regulations require that commercial fishing buoys be topped by flags with their owner's name.

Commercial fishing: Fishing as a business, rather than as a sport or pastime.

Crib: The box of net at the end of a trap net, into which fish swim and are trapped.

Dip net: A small, hand-held net used to pass fish between nets or containers.

Drag net: A net drawn along a river or lake bottom to catch fish.

Fish house: A fish wholesale business, to which commercial fishermen bring and sell their catches.

Fyke net: A bag-shaped net. An ancestor of the contemporary seine net.

Gill net: A net of lightweight material hung in the water from floats, which catches fish by the gills as they swim through it.

Hook-and-line fishing: Simple personal fishing with a rod and reel. *See also* Sport fishing.

Lead: A long length of net at the front end of a trap net, set across the path of fish so that they will swim along it into the crib.

Lifting nets: Raising nets from the water in order to remove fish from them, after which they are lowered back into the water.

Mesh size: The size of the "holes" in a net, measured in inches.

Pound net: A net structure held upright by stakes, usually in shallower water, to trap fish. An ancestor of the contemporary trap net.

Pulling nets: Removing nets from the water for repair or storage.

Seine net: A long net with a bag at its center, suspended in the water and then drawn into a progressively tighter circle to trap fish in the bag. Seining can be done from a boat or from shore; the latter technique is used on Lake Erie.

Setting nets: Placing nets in the water for fishing.

Sport fishing: Generally, fishing as a pastime. Sport fishing may be done on a small, inexpensive scale or with expensive boats and equipment. When commercial fishermen use this term, they usually mean the expensive version; otherwise, they usually say "hook-and-line."

Trap net: A net structure held upright with floats at the top and weights at the bottom, usually in deeper water, to trap fish.

Trash fish: Fish species that are not eaten by humans, which therefore bring lower prices at market.

Trawling: Fishing by dragging a line or net along or near the bottom.

Trotline: A fishing line strung across a river or stream, with other, hooked lines suspended from it.

Walleye: The most popular sport fish on the lake, sold at fish markets and restaurants as "pickerel." Ohio commercial fishermen have been prohibited from taking this fish since 1972; the walleye sold in Ohio is generally imported from Canada.

Weir: A handmade fence, usually of wood, set into a stream for catching fish.

Bibliography

Abrahams, Roger. 1972. Personal power and social restraint in the definition of folklore. In *Toward new perspectives in folklore,* ed. Americo Paredes and Richard Bauman, 16–30. Austin: Univ. of Texas Press.

———. 1976. The complex relations of simple forms. In *Folklore genres,* ed. Dan Ben-Amos, 193–214. Austin: Univ. of Texas Press.

Acheson, James M. 1981. Anthropology of fishing. *Annual review of anthropology* 10:275–316.

Andersen, Raoul, ed. 1979. *North Atlantic maritime cultures: Anthropological essays on changing adaptation.* The Hague: Mouton.

Andersen, Raoul, and Cato Wadel, eds. 1972. *North Atlantic fishermen: Anthropological essays on modern fishing.* Newfoundland: Memorial Univ. of Newfoundland.

Applegate, Vernon C., and Harry D. Van Meter. 1970. *A brief history of commercial fishing in Lake Erie.* U.S. Fish and Wildlife Services Fisheries Leaflet no. 630. Washington, D.C.

Atkinson, John W., ed. 1958. *Motives in fantasy, action, and society: A method of assessment and study.* Princeton, NJ: Van Nostrand.

Babcock, Barbara. 1984. The story in the story: metanarration in folk narrative. In *Verbal art as performance,* ed. Richard Bauman, 61–79. Prospect Heights, IL: Waveland Press.

Barnes, Mark. 1983. *History of commercial fishing on Lake Erie.* Columbus, OH: Ohio Sea Grant.

Bassett, Fletcher S. 1885. *Legends and superstitions of the sea and of sailors: In all lands and at all times.* London: Sampson Low, Marston, Searle, and Rivington.

Bauman, Richard. 1971. Differential identity and the social base of folklore. *Journal of American folklore* 84:31–41.

Bausinger, Hermann. 1958. Strukturen des alltäglichen Erzählens. *Fabula* 1:239–54.

Beck, Horace P. 1957. *The folklore of Maine.* Philadelphia: J. B. Lippincott.

Boatright, Mody. 1961. *Folk laughter on the American frontier*. New York: Collier Books.

———. 1963. *Folklore of the oil industry*. Dallas: Southern Methodist Univ. Press.

Boatright, Mody C., and William A. Owens. 1970. *Tales from the derrick floor: A people's history of the oil industry*. Lincoln: Univ. of Nebraska Press.

Botkin, Benjamin A., and Alvin Harlow, eds. 1953. *A treasury of railroad folklore*. New York: Crown Publishers.

Butcher, David. 1980. *The trawlermen*. Reading, Eng.: Tops'l Books.

Byington, Robert H., ed. 1978. *Working Americans: Contemporary approaches to occupational folklife*. *Western folklore* 17.

———. 1984. Introduction to folklore. In *Teaching folklore*, ed. Bruce Jackson, 18–32. Buffalo: Documentary Research.

Chowning, Larry S. 1983. *Barcat skipper: Tales of a Tangier Island waterman*. Centreville, MD: Tidewater Publishers.

Clifford, Harold B. 1974. *Charlie York: Maine coast fisherman*. Camden, ME: International Marine Publishing.

Cochrane, Tim. 1983. Isle Royale commercial fishermen's authority stories: An indication of changing environmental perception. Paper presented at the annual meeting of the American Folklore Society, Nashville.

Curry, Jane. 1983. *The river's in my blood: Riverboat pilots tell their stories*. Lincoln: Univ. of Nebraska Press.

Degh, Linda. 1972. Folk narrative. In *Folklore and folklife: An introduction*, ed. Richard M. Dorson, 53–83. Chicago: Univ. of Chicago Press.

Dolby-Stahl, Sandra K. 1985. A literary folkloristic methodology for the study of meaning in personal narrative. *Journal of folklore research* 22:45–69.

Dorson, Richard M. 1959. *American folklore*. Chicago: Univ. of Chicago Press.

———. 1964. *Buying the wind: Regional folklore in the United States*. Chicago: Univ. of Chicago Press.

———. 1968. Legends and tall tales. In *Our living traditions: An introduction to American folklore*, ed. Tristram Potter Coffin, 154–69. New York: Basic Books.

Dundes, Alan. 1962. From etic to emic units in the structural study of folktales. *Journal of American folklore* 75:95–105.

———. 1983. Defining identity through folklore. In *Identity: Personal and socio-cultural, a symposium*, ed. Anita Jacobson-Widding, 235–61. Uppsala: Uppsala Studies in Cultural Anthropology no. 5.

Erikson, Erik. 1959. *Identity and the life cycle*. New York: International Universities Press.

Faris, James C. 1972. *Cat Harbour: A Newfoundland fishing settlement*. St. John's: Memorial Univ. of Newfoundland.

Fields, Mary C. 1974. The view from the water table: Folklore of the offshore oilfield workers. *Mid-South folklore* 2:63–76.

Forrest, John. 1988. *Lord I'm coming home: Everyday aesthetics in Tidewater North Carolina*. Ithaca: Cornell Univ. Press.

Fricke, Peter H., ed. 1973. *Seafarer and community*. London: Croom Helm.

Gilmore, Janet C. 1983. Fishermen stereotypes and the fishing community. Paper presented at the annual meeting of the American Folklore Society, Nashville.

———. 1986. *The world of the Oregon fishboat: A study in maritime folklife.* Ann Arbor: UMI Research Press.

Goodenough, Ward Hunt. 1963. *Cooperation in change.* New York: Russell Sage Foundation.

Green, Archie. 1972. *Only a miner: Studies in recorded coal mining songs.* Urbana: Univ. of Illinois Press.

Green, Ben. 1985. *Finest kind: A celebration of a Florida fishing village.* Macon, GA: Mercer Univ. Press.

Gunda, Bela, ed. 1984. *The fishing culture of the world: Studies in ethnology, cultural ecology and folklore.* 2 vols. Budapest: Akademiai Kiado.

Harper, Douglas. 1987. *Working knowledge: Skill and community in a small shop.* Chicago: Univ. of Chicago Press.

Hasslof, Olof, Henning Henningsen, and Arne Emil Christiansen, eds. 1972. *Ships and shipyards, sailors and fishermen: Introduction to maritime ethnology.* Copenhagen: Rosenkilde and Bagger.

Ives, Edward D. 1978. *Joe Scott: The woodsman-songmaker.* Urbana: Univ. of Illinois Press.

Jacobson-Widding, Anita. 1983. Introduction. In *Identity: Personal and socio-cultural, a symposium,* 13–33. *See* Dundes 1983.

Jansen, Wm. Hugh. 1959. The esoteric-exoteric factor in folklore. *Fabula: journal of folktale studies* 2:205–11.

Jolles, Andre. 1965. *Einfache formen: Legende, sage, mythe, ratsel, spruch, kasus, memorabile, märchen, witz.* Tübingen: M. Niemeyer.

Johnson, Paula J., ed. 1988. *Working the water: The commercial fisheries of Maryland's Patuxent River.* Charlottesville: Univ. Press of Virginia.

Korson, George. 1938. *Minstrels of the mine patch.* Philadelphia: Univ. of Pennsylvania Press.

Labov, William. 1972. *Language in the inner city.* Philadelphia: Univ. of Pennsylvania Press.

Landberg, Leif. 1973, 1979. *A bibliography for the anthropological study of fishing industries and maritime communities* and *Supplement.* Kingston: Univ. of Rhode Island International Center for Marine Resources Development.

Leary, James P. 1984. Style in jocular communication: From the cultural to the personal. *Journal of folklore research* 21:29–46.

Liebkind, Karmela. 1983. Dimensions of identity in multiple group allegiance. In *Identity: Personal and socio-cultural, a symposium,* 187–204. *See* Dundes 1983.

Lomax, John A. 1910. *Cowboy songs and other frontier ballads.* New York: Macmillan.

Lummis, Trevor. 1985. *Occupation and society: The East Anglia fisherman, 1880–1914.* Cambridge: Cambridge Univ. Press.

Lund, Jens. 1983. Fishing as a folk occupation in the lower Ohio Valley. Ph.D. diss., Indiana University.

McCarl, Robert S. 1978. Occupational folklife: A theoretical hypothesis. *Western folklore* 37:145–60.

———. 1985. *The District of Columbia fire fighters' project, a case study in occupational folklife.* Washington, DC: Smithsonian Institution Press.

McClelland, David C. 1961. *The achieving society.* Princeton, NJ: Van Nostrand.

Malinowski, Bronislaw. 1948. *Magic, science and religion and other essays.* Garden City, NY: Doubleday.

Matthiessen, Peter. 1986. *Men's lives: The surfmen and baymen of the South Fork.* New York: Random House.

Mullen, Patrick B. 1978a. American folklife and *The grapes of wrath. Journal of American culture* 1:742–53.

———. 1978b. *I heard the old fishermen say: Folklore of the Texas Gulf Coast.* Austin: Univ. of Texas Press.

Neumann, Siegfried. 1967. Arbeitserinnerungen als erzahlungsinhalt. *Deutsches jahrbuch für volkskunde* 12:179–90.

Orbach, Michael K. 1977. *Hunters, seamen and entrepreneurs: The tuna seinermen of San Diego.* Berkeley: Univ. of California Press.

Orbach, Michael K., and Valerie R. Harper, eds. 1979. *United States fisheries systems and social science: A bibliography of work and directory of researchers.* Washington, DC: National Marine Fisheries Service.

Pike, Kenneth. 1954–60. *Language in relation to a unified theory of the structures of human behavior.* Glendale: Summer Institute of Linguistics.

Poggie, John, and Carl Gersuny. 1972. Risk and ritual: An interpretation of fishermen's folklore in a New England community. *Journal of American folklore* 85:66–72.

———. 1974. *Fishermen of Galilee: The human ecology of a New England coastal community.* Kingston: Univ. of Rhode Island, Sea Grant.

Robinson, John A. 1981. Personal narratives reconsidered. *Journal of American folklore* 94:58–85.

Santino, Jack. 1978. Characteristics of occupational narratives. *Western folklore* 37:199–212.

———. 1983. Miles of smiles, years of struggle: The negotiation of black occupational identity through personal experience narrative. *Journal of American folklore* 96:393–412.

Scrivo, Bill. 1986. Taking in Old Jib. *Ohio magazine* 9(3):9–10.

Smith, Barbara Herrnstein. 1980. Narrative versions, narrative theories. *Critical inquiry* 7:213–36.

Smith, M. Estellie. 1977. *Those who live from the sea: A story in maritime anthropology.* St. Paul: West Publishing.

Spacks, Patricia Meyer. 1976. *Imagining a self: Autobiography and novel in eighteenth-century England.* Cambridge: Harvard Univ. Press.

Spicer, Edward H. 1971. Persistent cultural systems: a comparative study of identity systems that can adapt to contrasting environments. *Science* 174:795–800.

Stahl, Sandra K.D. 1975. The local character anecdote. *Genre* 8:283–302.

———. 1977a. The oral personal narrative in its generic context. *Fabula* 18:18–39.

———. 1977b. The personal narrative as folklore. *Journal of the folklore institute* 14:9–30.

Sydow, Carl Wilhelm von. 1948. *Selected papers on folklore*. Copenhagen: Rosenkilde and Bagger.

Tanner, Tony. 1965. *The reign of wonder: Naivety and reality in American literature*. Cambridge: Cambridge Univ. Press.

Thompson, Ellery. 1950. *Draggerman's haul: The personal history of a Connecticut fishing captain*. New York: Viking Press.

Thompson, Paul, Tony Wailey, and Trevor Lummis. 1985. *Living the fishing*. London: Routledge and Kegan Paul.

Titon, Jeff Todd. 1980. The life story. *Journal of American folklore* 93:276–92.

Toelken, Barre. 1979. *The dynamics of folklore*. Boston: Houghton Mifflin.

Tunstall, Jeremy. 1962. *The fishermen*. London: MacGibbon and Lee.

Van Winkle, Ted. 1975. *Fred Boynton, lobsterman, New Harbor, Maine*. Camden, ME: International Marine Publishing.

Vogt, Evon Z. 1955. *Modern homesteaders: The life of a twentieth-century frontier community*. Cambridge: Belknap Press of Harvard Univ. Press.

Warner, William. 1976. *Beautiful swimmers*. Boston: Little, Brown.

Wilbur, Richard, and Ernest Wentworth. 1986. *Silver harvest: the Fundy weirmen's story*. Frederickton, New Brunswick: Fiddlehead Poetry Books and Goose Lane Editions.

Wilson, William A. 1988. The deeper necessity: Folklore and the humanities. *Journal of American folklore* 101:156–67.

Wolfson, Nessa. 1976. Speech events and natural speech: Some implications for sociolinguistic methodology. *Language in society* 5:189–209.

Zavalloni, Marisa. 1973. Social identity: Perspectives and prospects. *Social science information* 12:65–91.

———. 1983. Ego-ecology: the study of the interaction between social and personal identities. In *Identity: personal and socio-cultural, a symposium*, 205–33. *See* Dundes 1983.

Index

A Note on the Authors

Timothy C. Lloyd is Director of the Traditional and Ethnic Arts Program at the Ohio Arts Council, Executive Secretary-Treasurer of the American Folklore Society, and author, producer, and curator of works on the traditional arts.

Patrick B. Mullen is Professor of English at Ohio State University, author of *I Heard the Old Fishermen Say: Folklore of the Texas Gulf Coast* (Texas, 1978), and has written many articles and reviews in folklore and American literature.

DATE DUE